PAPERS AND CORRESPONDENCE
OF
WILLIAM STANLEY JEVONS

Volume VI

PAPERS AND CORRESPONDENCE
OF
WILLIAM STANLEY JEVONS

Volume VI
LECTURES ON POLITICAL ECONOMY
1875–1876

EDITED BY

R. D. COLLISON BLACK

in association with the Royal Economic Society

First published 1977 by
THE MACMILLAN PRESS LTD
London and Basingstoke
Associated companies in New York
Dublin Melbourne Johannesburg and Madras

SBN 333 10258 4

Printed in Great Britain by
UNWIN BROTHERS LIMITED
THE GRESHAM PRESS, OLD WOKING, SURREY
A MEMBER OF THE STAPLES PRINTING GROUP

CONTENTS

A complete index to the *Papers and Correspondence*, *Lectures*, and *Papers on Political Economy* will be contained in Volume VII.

PREFACE

In the Preface to Volume I (pp. xi–xii) it was stated that Volume IV would contain the text of a series of lectures on Political Economy delivered by W. S. Jevons to the day class at Owens College during the academic year 1875–6, together with the text of a number of economic papers by him either previously unpublished or not included in either *Investigations* or *Methods*, a selection of entries from the diaries which he kept between 1856 and 1860, a list of his writings derived from a notebook in which he himself entered details of his publications, a selection of examination papers taken or set by Jevons, and a series of reviews of the *Theory of Political Economy*.

For the reasons explained in the Preface to Volume III (p. xvii) it has proved necessary to divide this collection of material into two volumes. The present volume contains only the notes of the 1875–6 lectures, and the remaining items appear in Volume VII. At first glance it may appear that the contents of these two volumes, and of Volume VII in particular, represent a very miscellaneous collection of Jevonsiana. In fact the two volumes have a unifying theme and purpose. The place of Jevons in the history of economic thought as a pioneer of the 'marginal revolution' is not in doubt, and that position was established by his published works. But Jevons was also one of the first of the great English economists to be a full-time academic and thus he was something of a pioneer in the 'professionalisation' of economics. About this important aspect of his career much less has previously been known, for his published works provide little information on it. Fortunately a considerable amount of relevant material was preserved in the Jevons Papers and most of it is now made accessible for the first time in these two volumes.

Perhaps one of the most important questions which can be raised about an academic economist is 'how did he present his subject to his pupils?' Yet very little material is available to enable historians of economic ideas to answer such a question about leading figures in the development of the science. Some have published texts, such as Walras's *Elements*, which retain something of the original form of classroom presentation but were subjected to an uncertain amount of revision and polishing by the author. Notes taken as the lectures were delivered are more seldom found; the best-known examples, separated in time by more than a century and a half, are Adam Smith's *Lectures on Justice, Police, Revenue and Arms*[1] and Wesley Mitchell's Lecture Notes on *Types of Economic Theory*.[2] It is therefore of particular interest to have another set of such lecture notes, showing how one of the founders of neo-classical economics presented his subject to undergraduates a century ago.

The notes which are published in this volume were taken down, apparently in longhand, by Harold Rylett, a student in the course on Political Economy given by Jevons during his last year as Professor at Owens College, Manchester. Some two years later Rylett made a fair copy of his notes and sent them to Jevons.[3] Jevons feared that his lectures 'had undergone some improvement in the process' adding that 'it is well known how much of the oratory we read is due to the reporters'. This is one of the problems which faces both editor and reader of such a set of notes. In Rylett's notes some of the oratory we read is due to Rylett rather than Jevons, but the result was not always an improvement. Sometimes he missed passages in a lecture or could not reconstruct them when he came to copy them out; at other times he made mistakes and did not recognise them as such afterwards. In editing the manuscript I have preserved the original form as far as is consistent with making the text readable, but have indicated all the points where it can be proved that Rylett misreported Jevons and have supplied what would appear to be the correct reading.

Chronologically, these lectures were given when Jevons had already published the first edition of the *Theory of Political Economy* and *Money and the Mechanism of Exchange* but had still to write the *Primer of Political Economy* and begin his *Principles of Economics*. Seen in this context, they throw an interesting light on the development of his economic ideas. In broad outline, the pattern of the Lectures is similar to that of the *Primer*, but the treatment, especially of value, is more advanced and indeed covers most of the ground treated in the *Theory of Political Economy*. Yet there is a notable difference from that book in the amount of factual and comparative material introduced, an approach which Jevons evidently intended to develop further in his unfinished *Principles*.

Money and credit, both domestic and international, take a prominent place in these lectures; but in view of Jevons's stature as a value theorist it

---

[1] Edited by Edwin Cannan (Oxford, 1896). W. R. Scott ascribed these lectures to 1762–3, but the recent discovery of another set of manuscript notes for the session 1762–3 has led Professor Meek and Mr Skinner to suggest that the 'Cannan notes' actually relate to lectures delivered in 1763–4. See R. L. Meek and A. S. Skinner, 'The Development of Adam Smith's ideas on the Division of Labour', *Economic Journal*, 83 (1973) 1094–116.

[2] Wesley C. Mitchell, *Types of Economic Theory*, edited with an Introduction by Joseph Dorfman (1967). An earlier mimeographed version of the lectures, which were delivered in 1934–5, was published in 1949.

[3] See Letter 521, Vol. IV, p. 241.

is curious to note that he did not take his students through the analysis of international values at all. The two lectures devoted to a largely historical account of commercial fluctuations show both the extent of his empirical researches and the development of his interest in the explanation of the decennial cycle, but the students of 1875–6 seem to have been given no hint of the sun-spot hypothesis which Jevons had first put forward before the British Association in August 1875.[4]

According to Keynes the effect on Jevons's mind of the 'sad reverse' which he suffered in the Political Economy examinations at University College London in 1860, as a result of putting forward his own theories, was 'curious':

> The students whom he had to teach when he became Professor at Owens College were accustomed to sit for the London examinations. As he thought it would be unfair to expose his own pupils to the rebuff he himself had suffered, his conscience did not allow him to teach them his own characteristic doctrine. His courses at Manchester were mainly confined to an exposition of Mill. I had long ago heard this from my father, and how his repression of his own theories had brought his feeling against Mill to boiling point. A book of careful lecture notes taken down by a member of his class, which I lately came across, confirms that this was so.[5]

Since Keynes was given access to the Jevons Papers by Miss H. W. Jevons and since no other notes by students are known to exist, it seems almost certain that Keynes must have been referring to Rylett's notes, even though these were copied out on separate sheets, not in a book. If so, it would seem that Keynes's examination of them must have been cursory, and made with his preconceptions in mind. For a careful reading of the notes will show that Jevons was describing his teaching with complete accuracy when he wrote to W. H. Brewer in 1873: 'I have generally followed somewhat the order of subjects in Mill's Pol. Econ. in perfect independence, however, of his views and methods when desirable.'[6] This 'perfect independence' extended to a full discussion of the theories of utility, disutility and exchange along the lines of the *Theory of Political Economy,* together with a sharp and telling attack on Mill's famous proposition that 'demand for commodities is not demand for labour'. It is hard to reconcile this with Keynes's picture of a frustrated teacher repressing his own theories.

Keynes did indeed allow that

---

[4] Cf. 'The Solar Period and the Price of Corn', *Investigations*, p. 194.
[5] *Collected Writings of J. M. Keynes*, vol. x, *Essays in Biography*, pp. 137–8.
[6] Letter 364, Vol. IV; p. 23.

some qualification to the above is suggested by the following note appended by Jevons in his list of mathematico-economic books: 'From about the year 1863 I regularly employed intersecting curves to illustrate the determination of the market price in my lectures at Owens College'.[7] The lecture notes referred to above do, indeed, include a sketch of a demand curve, but the accompanying text contains no reference to the marginal principle.[8]

Yet this too is very difficult to reconcile with what is actually to be found in Rylett's notes. Curves there are, indeed, but they are all, as would be expected with Jevons, utility curves and not demand curves, while the accompanying text contains virtually as much reference to the marginal principle as did the *Theory of Political Economy*.

In this instance, however, Jevons's own statement about his lectures is as puzzling as that of Keynes. 'Intersecting curves' might indeed be interpreted as meaning the superimposed utility curves for two commodities used to illustrate the theory of exchange in *Theory of Political Economy*,[9] which construction Jevons does appear to have explained to the class which Rylett attended. Yet the context of his remark strongly implies that he meant demand and supply curves similar to those used by Fleeming Jenkin; if that is so he did not present such curves in the lectures of 1875–6 and the only possible explanation seems to lie in Jevons's other comment that 'the relative amount of attention given to the different parts [of the course] . . . has in my own case varied much from year to year'.[10]

For help in dealing with the manuscript material included in this volume and Volume VII I am grateful to Dr Margaret Wright and Miss P. Mathieson of the John Rylands Library of the University of Manchester, and to the Librarian of Chetham's Library, Manchester, for information relating to John Mills's paper on 'Credit Cycles', referred to by Jevons in Lecture XXII. My thanks are also due to my colleagues Professor J. A. Faris and Dr W. A. Gabbey, who assisted me to place some of the references to Bacon and Kant, and to Mrs M. Y. Keary, Readers' Services Librarian, Civil Service Department, Whitehall, for information relating to the career of T. C. Banfield.

Queen's University, Belfast   R. D. COLLISON BLACK
November 1975

[7] *T.P.E.*, p. 333.
[8] Keynes, loc. cit.
[9] *T.P.E.*, p. 97.
[10] Cf. Letter 364, loc. cit.

LIST OF ABBREVIATIONS
used throughout the volumes

Relating to Jevons material

LJ — *Letters and Journal of W. Stanley Jevons,* edited by his wife (1886).

LJN — Previously published in LJ; manuscript not now in Jevons Papers, or other known location.

LJP — Previously published in LJ, but only in part; fuller text now given from the orginal manuscript in the Jevons Papers or other indicated location.

WM — From a manuscript made available by Dr Wolfe Mays, University of Manchester.

Investigations — *Investigations in Currency and Finance,* by W. Stanley Jevons. Edited, with an Introduction, by H. S. Foxwell (1884). All page references to first edition.

Methods — *Methods of Social Reform and other papers,* by W. Stanley Jevons (1883).

T.P.E. — *The Theory of Political Economy* by W. Stanley Jevons (1st ed. 1871, 4th ed. 1911). All page references to fourth edition, unless otherwise stated.

Relating to other material

BM — British Museum, London (now British Library).

FW — Fonds Walras, Bibliothèque Cantonale de Lausanne.

HLRS — Herschel Letters, Royal Society, London

JRSS — *Journal of the London* (later *Royal*) *Statistical Society.*

KCP — Palgrave Papers in the Library of King's College, Cambridge.

LSE — London School of Economics, British Library of Political and Economic Science.

MA — Archives of Macmillan & Co. Ltd.

NYPL — New York Public Library.

RDF — From a manuscript made available by Mr R. D. Freeman.

TLJM — Isabel Mills, *From Tinder Box to the 'Larger Light'. Threads from the Life of John Mills, Banker* (Manchester, 1899).

Walras Correspondence — *Correspondence of Léon Walras and Related Papers* edited by William Jaffé (3 vols, Amsterdam, 1965).

Figures following any of these abbreviations denote page numbers.

LECTURES

LECTURE I

DEFINITIONS OF POLITICAL ECONOMY

Gentlemen – I recommend as a book to be referred to, Adam Smith's Wealth of Nations,[1] because I am more & more convinced that it contains probably more truth & less error than any other book on the same subject, altho' it still contains a considerable amount of error. But those parts which are true are so admirably written, so clear & classical, that I think it is the best text book we can select. Of course, Mill's Political Economy[2] is considered the leading work on the subject, & I shall certainly ask you to read considerable portions of it. Mill's Political Economy is disfigured by a series of fallacies, & these I shall have to point out to you from time to time. A great part of the work is erroneous – almost more than in Adam Smith's Wealth of Nations. So I don't wish to take Mill as a standard text book. There are several other books. One is Senior's Manual, originally published in the Encyclopaedia Metropolitana, but it has been republished in a very convenient form, price about 4/6d.[3] Now the earlier part of this is the best piece of writing on the subject of political economy, I believe, ever written – that is to say, just the introduction and the skeleton of the subject, which it begins with. And Senior is probably the soundest political economist that ever wrote, or taken with Malthus certainly. [Meaning: "certainly taken with Malthus."][4] If the remainder of this book were as good as the beginning, there wd. be nothing better wanted in the way of a text book. Unfortunately it falls off, gets into discussions & digressions, so that I am prevented fr. using this as a skeleton of our course. Some students have a great opn. of Fawcetts Manual,[5] & Fawcett is no doubt a great man; and if any student wishes to read his manual he will find it a very clear & readable digest of Mill's system; but at the same

[1] Jevons's letter of 22 November 1879 to H. S. Foxwell suggests that the actual edition of Smith's *Wealth of Nations* recommended to his students was the reprint of the fifth edition, published as one of 'Murray's Choice Reprints' in 1874. See Vol. V, Letter 631A, nn. 2–4, p. 81.

[2] It is not clear what edition Jevons used. All page references here are to *The Collected Works of John Stuart Mill*, vols II and III, *Principles of Political Economy*, edited by J. M. Robson (Toronto, 1965).

[3] Nassau W. Senior (1790–1864), *An Outline of the Science of Political Economy* (1836); page references are to the reprint of the seventh edition published in the Library of Economics Series, 1938. The work was originally published as the article 'Political Economy' in the *Encyclopaedia Metropolitana*, 25 vols (1845) VI, 129–224, and the first separate edition of it was a direct reprint, paginated as in the *Encyclopaedia*.

[4] This and subsequent insertions by Rylett are indicated by square brackets.

[5] Henry Fawcett, *A Manual of Political Economy* (1863). See Vol. III, Letter 190, n. 2, p. 37, cf. also Letter 271, n. 2, p. 139.

time it contains comparatively few opinions but those of Mill. It has been
*publicly*⁶ described as "Mill & Water",⁷ and it is not altogether an inapt
expression. But it is much simpler & more readable than Mill: so some
students like it very much. At the same time, I rather prefer that you
should read portions of the original. In fact, Fawcett himself remarks that
those who wd. read Mill need not read his own book. Then, I shall refer to
a portion of my own theory of the science, and on "money" I shall have to
                    a work
refer to one just published of my own. Other books will only be referred to
on special points – such as Whateley's [*sic*] introductory lecture.⁸

Take notice – the subject is informal in many parts & so cannot be
tested in the same way as in logic – so I urge you to take full & concise
notes.

The name of our science is a very awkward one – political, an
adjective, and economy, a substantive noun. Some people think we had
better call it Economy simply – "political" superfluous if not erroneous.
Others have proposed various greek or latin names, such as plutology, the
science of wealth; χρηματιστική the science of exchangeable articles;
καταλλακτικη the science of exchangeable things, but they come to much
the same thing in the end. But it may be considered to be a rule that when
once a name is thoroughly established & recognised as definitely applied
to a particular branch of science there is more harm in changing it than in
keeping an awkward name. Everyone knows that political economy is
applied to the science of wealth – so that there is no more harm in it than
simply a superfluous word. But probably none of these names have
succeeded in supplanting it & don't seem likely to do. Now, looking at the
word, economy comes from the Greek οἰκονομία, meaning the regulation of a household, οικος, a house, & νέμω, I distribute, regulate.
The Greeks had a verb οἰκονομὲω and οἰκογομικός or οἰκονόμος
meant a manager, or one who exercises economy. Even as far back as
Plato the word οἰκονομία was applied to the management of the State.
Almost all expressions you will find out are derived by some kind of
analogy. Accordingly the word Economy has come to be widened so as to
mean any kind of regulation in any particular department – economy of

[* ? popularly]   (H. R.)

⁶ Throughout the original manuscript, Rylett placed asterisks at passages about which he was
uncertain, or on which he wished to expand. In this text comments by Rylett are distinguished by the
initials 'H. R'.

⁷ According to Jacob Viner, a similar title was given by him and his fellow-students to the first
college course in economics which he took, about 1910, and for which J. S. Mill's *Principles* and F. A.
Walker's *Political Economy* were the prescribed texts. Cf. J. Viner, *The Long View and the Short* (Glencoe,
Illinois, 1958) p. 329.

⁸ Richard Whately, *Introductory Lectures on Political Economy delivered in Easter Term, 1831* (1832). Cf.
Vol. I, pp. 6, n. 2, and 157, n. 4.

printing office etc., meaning a minute regulation of affairs, especially of finance, the best spending of the funds. Now the use of the adjective πολιτικὸs specialises it to the economy of the State, which among the Greeks was simply a town or πόλιs.

Some writers have said political economy might be defined. James Mill says political economy is to the State what domestic economy is to the family;[9] but that would be very misleading if we took it to mean a mere analogy, because for instance domestic economy does not include always the production of wealth. Domestic economy is the successful expenditure of the household revenue, whereas political economy looks at least as much to the production of wealth as to its consumption, if not more.

I don't know that properly speaking we ought to begin with a definition of the science. I believe the truer logical method is to allow a science to become whatever a logical growth makes it. That is the doctrine of Professor* *Martineau* – that no science shd. be restricted in its growth by a definition, – that it ought to be allowed to collect around it all facts of a similar nature.[10] I perfectly agree with that, & therefore when we begin with a definition of the science, it is not because we want to restrict it or because we think it restricts it. It is only in a didactic way, because we want the shortest way to catch some idea of what it is. And if after having taken the definitions of other people we find that really we can include things excluded by them we shall throw their definitions aside.

Taking the definitions as merely didactic we find some brief extracts in the beginning of Senior's Manual.[11] We begin with some of the French writers who profess that political economy shd. produce all happiness. But all sciences do what M. de la Riviere say[s] this of economy does.[12]

Sismondi, an Italian writer, considers that political economy treats of "the physical welfare of man, so far as it can be the work of government".[13]

---

[9] James Mill (1773–1836), *Elements of Political Economy* (1821) p. 1.

[* I doubt whether I caught this exactly]   (H. R.)

[10] James Martineau, 'Plea for Philosophical Studies', an address presented in February 1854 on taking the Chair of Philosophy in Manchester New College, London. See Martineau, *Essays, Reviews and Addresses*, 4 vols (1891) IV, 26–7. Cf. Vol. II, Letter 147, n. 4, p. 421.

[11] Senior, op. cit., pp. 1–2.

[12] Pierre François Joachim Henri Le Mercier de la Rivière (1720?–93), *L'Ordre Naturel et Essentiel des Sociétés Politiques* (1767), Discours Préliminaire, p. vi. Senior gave an extract from a statement by Le Mercier which Jevons here paraphrased further; the result is a caricature of the original meaning. Le Mercier wrote: 'Mes recherches . . . m'ont convaincu qu'il existe un ordre naturel pour le gouvernement des hommes réunis en société; un ordre qui nous assure nécessairement toute la felicité temporelle à laquelle nous sommes appellés pendant notre séjour sur la terre. . . .' In translating part of this Senior had at least commented that 'the earlier writers who assumed the name Political Economists avowedly treated not of Wealth but of Government'.

[13] Jean Charles Léonard Simonde de Sismondi (1773–1842), Italian writer on economics and

Another writer, Storch, says that P.E. is the science of the natural laws which determine [the][14] prosperity of nations.[15]

These are all foreign writers. But English writers have, generally speaking, restricted the subject more. The welfare or prosperity of a nation includes all sources of welfare and prosperity and therefore includes all moral and political causes or even religious causes. A nation may enjoy happiness that is not very rich, certainly, may have a certain moderate independence; and the political constitution of society is a matter greatly affecting its welfare independently of wealth. Therefore, if we take the definition of Sismondi or Storch P.E. would really include the whole of the social sciences – if not physical science. Therefore, we may fairly consider that the Eng. writers are correct in restricting political economy to one branch, one source of the welfare of nations, and that source is wealth, or, as I shall analyse it, Utility.

A great many writers have in slightly varied words defined economy or the science of wealth, and Smith calls his work the Wealth of Nations. Mill says "Writers on Political Economy profess to teach or investigate the nature of wealth and the laws of its production and distribution, including directly or remotely the operation of all the causes by which the condition of mankind or of any society of human beings, in respect of this universal object of human desire, is made prosperous or the reverse."[16]

Other definitions are only verbally different, as for instance that of McCullough[sic] which says it is "the Science of the laws which regulate the production, accumulation, distribution and consumption of those articles or products that are necessary useful or agreeable to man and possess exchangeable value."[17] We shall soon see that that really comes to the same thing, for these things are wealth.

Senior's definition is to the same effect. He says it is the "Science which treats of the nature, the production, and distribution of wealth."[18]

The variations of definition are not essential among Eng. writers.

Before we go on to investigate what wealth is, I will just enter into a

---

medieval history. This quotation is taken from his *Political Economy* (1815; reprinted New York, 1966) p. 1 and reads in full: 'The physical well-being of man, so far as it can be produced by his government, is the object of Political Economy.'

[14] Omitted in the original manuscript.

[15] Heinrich Friedrich von Storch (1766–1835), a German who made his career in Russia, whose work in economics follows Smithian lines. This definition is taken from *Cours d'économie politique, ou exposition des principes qui déterminent la prosperité des nations . . . avec des notes explicatives et critiques par J. B. Say,* 5 vols (Paris, 1823–4) I, 21; see Senior, op. cit., p. 1.

[16] Mill, *Principles*, p. 3.

[17] John Ramsay McCulloch (1789–1864), *The Principles of Political Economy*, fifth edition (Edinburgh, 1864; reprinted New York, 1965) p. 1. The last part of the sentence reads ' . . . products that are necessary, useful, or agreeable to man, and which at the same time possess exchangeable value'.

[18] Senior, op. cit., p. 1.

defence of the subject. It is requisite to do so on account of the persistent absurdity of a large number of writers and speakers who continually abuse our science. It is called a dismal science.[19] It has been called mechanical, hard hearted, miserable and even wicked. There is a certain class of sentimental writers who think political economists the greatest brutes in the world because they look only to wealth and would let a person die rather than relieve him. They think that a moral science ought to be moral in all kinds of sympathies and feelings, duties etc. But this is a most superficial and absurd objection, for this reason, that you cannot take the whole of the moral sciences into any one science, any more than you can take all the physical sciences into chemistry or astronomy. You might as well object to the astronomer for regarding the planets as mere matter. You might say "Why does he look merely to the theory of gravitation when he knows that the substance of the planet has got chemical and other qualities." But then we should never get on in physical science unless we had division of labour. Take iron itself. Iron may be regarded in a great many different lights, e.g. in a mechanical light. We may regard electricity and magnetism. Other substances are regarded from an optical point of view and you cannot have all sciences treated the same unless you roll them into one. Exactly the same applies to this science. We may be just, and we may take care of our rights and political power and our *health** . In short, any particular person must be regarded as governed by various considerations of which wealth is only one. But then there are principles governing the accumulation of wealth. These principles are totally different from the principles of morals. A very good illustration of this was given by Whatly (who wrote the Introductory lecture). He says that such an objection to political economy is very like objecting to mathematicians that they keep merely to accounts, or against grammarians for investigating no subject but language. And then he illustrates very well the place which P.E. takes in practice – because in other cases no other science gives absolute and independent advice, as it were. The science of medicine more or less supposes that there is a practice of medicine – it is commonplace for a physician to judge what is best for his patient. For instance a physician says that sea air will benefit his patient and says "you must go to the sea". But do you necessarily go to the sea? In various ways you might be in a position in which the physician's advice would have no power over you. Whether you are to go or not is to be a balance of very complicated considerations.[20]

This is precisely the position of political economy as regards other

[19] Thomas Carlyle (1795–1881), 'The Present Time', *Latter Day Pamphlets* (1872) p. 38.
[* ? wealth]   (H. R.)
[20] Whately, *Introductory Lectures,* second edition (1832), Lecture i, pp. 18–20.

instances. It undertakes to ascertain that to give money to other people tends to decrease the wealth of the community. As a gen. rule giving money in charity tends to slacken exertion, but I believe it is on that ground that political economy has been called cold hearted and wicked; but it does not follow that because it is against the accumulation of wealth that therefore it is never to be done. There may be humanitarian reasons, which notwithstanding may induce the state to give money to the poor, or lead some people to subscribe for charity, and that is perpetually done – only bear in mind the evil which thus results as regards the accumulation of wealth. It is well to know the effects even when we voluntarily agree to bad effects. It is the same with other things.

Accordingly the statesman is never to be bound by the dictum of a political economist, or a moralist, or any statist, or any lawyer, singly. The statesman is the one who balances the dicta of all social philosophers, you may say. He collects all the information on a subject that he can and by a kind of tact and good judgment says which will be the most expedient with regard to all possible considerations. I have no hesitation in saying that the relief of a famine stricken district, such as that of parts of India, is in one point of view an erroneous policy and almost impracticable to carry on. And then P.E. is called a wicked science because it even contemplates the death of a great number of people as the proper consequence of their position. But that is quite another thing from saying the Statesman is bound to let them perish. It might be the utmost wickedness and folly to let them do so, but not on the ground of wealth. I can't see any objection to this view. It seems to be exceedingly superficial of those who do object to this natural division of the subject.

Men have never succeeded in making any classification of moral sciences, but I might just enumerate them in this way.

Moral Philosophy: which treats of the character of men and the effects of actions on their characters.

Jurisprudence, which is difficult to define, but treats of a certain equality of rights.

Political philosophy, which treats of the distribution of power in a state.

Hygienic Science which treats of the prolongation of life.

Penal Jurisprudence, which treats of the punishment and prevention of crime.

A vast body of *Statistical,* or *Social* science. Anything referring to society is discussed under this head.

We shall begin next time with our own special subject of wealth. I shall start with Senior's definition – on p. 6. – and discuss what wealth really is.

LECTURE II

WEALTH

What is wealth? Mr. Mill has held that it is no part or no necessity of the science of P.E. to enter into definitions of metaphysical nicety where the ideas suggested by the term are already as determined as practical purposes require. And he thinks, as you will find on reading the Preliminary remarks, that everyone has a notion sufficiently correct for common purpose of what is meant by wealth.[1] But it may be shown, and perhaps I shall show you on a future day, that he himself takes the term wealth in at least four inconsistent or varying senses. Sometimes it is with him, what can be bought and sold, which would include labour, service of all kinds:—the very intellect of a man can be bought – e.g. to pay a fee to a barrister. At other times it is what can be accumulated. At other times it is the material product of the earth. We will go more fully at some other time into these definitions, but I think it best now to take the definition of Senior, because that is as accurate as circumstances will allow. You remember that Senior says that P.E. is the science which treats of the nature, production and distribution of wealth. Then by wealth, he says, we apprehend "all those things, and those things only which are *transferable,* which are *limited in supply,* and are directly or indirectly *productive of pleasure or preventive of pain*"[2] – three different qualities of wealth. This is the most clear definition I know in mental science. In the first place transferableness is requisite because otherwise things would be only, as it were, individual wealth. There are many things productive of pleasure and many preventive of pain, but if you can't give them over to other people, they would never be accounted as wealth. For instance if you have a good conscience that is productive of pleasure. Well, you cannot sell that. Or you may happen to have valuable friends. Now nobody can sell his friendships. Then, again, a person cannot transfer himself according to the English law. It is a fundamental principle of common law that you cannot sell yourself into slavery. But you can sell your service, and there does not appear to be any limit to the term for which a man can transfer his services. According to this, service would then be a part of wealth. This quality of transferableness only excludes those qualities of pleasure and pain which are purely individual and that cannot be turned over to anybody else. The illustration of that is what you call keepsakes, heirlooms, objects of fancy that nobody likes but the owner – a book, or a portrait of your ancestor – it may be a very ugly one – and many would sell it, but you won't.

[1] Mill, *Principles*, pp. 3–4.
[2] Senior, op. cit., p. 1. Rylett numbered these points '1, 2, 3' in the margin of the original manuscript.

Then wealth must be limited in supply – that is, you must have less of it than you would like to have. Of course everything is limited in supply, sooner or later, because the universe is finite. The amount of gold might be millions over what I know, but still some limited amount is in the world. So with limestones. There is nothing in the world immeasurable. Therefore everything is limited in supply so far, but then that is not the sense in which we take it. It must be limited in supply compared with human want. Now the air, in a sense, is not limited. For instance, in a great building or out of doors we have more air than we want, so that we have no need for more air. So with salt water at the sea side. And in other cases there is no limitation of supply e.g. sunlight in sunny countries – but here in Manchester it would seem to be limited at least sometimes. Common earth might seem to be very abundant, and poor earth very often is; but good land is *fortunately** very limited in supply. Thus those things cease to be wealth for the reason that further supply is no use. Indeed we sometimes have more than we can do with.

But we come to the third quality of wealth – that it must be either directly or indirectly productive of pleasure or preventive of pain. Directly means that something may be applied directly to our own persons. Wine, for instance. Things indirectly productive of pleasure are carpenters tools for instance. Playing a musical instrument would be direct.

Productive of pleasure or preventive of pain. – So far as I can see it is almost impossible to distinguish between them in detail. There are some cases more productive of pleasure – musical instruments for instance. There are other things that might be called purely preventive of pain, as, for instance, the forceps of a dentist cannot be said to produce any pleasure. They simply remove pain. In any other case it seems impossible to discriminate between them.

Now I introduce a term that shall simplify the matter and in place of directly or indirectly etc., we will use *utility*. So that wealth – transferable – limited in supply – possesses utility. Utility is to political economy what light is to optics. Indeed it is the very subject of it. So that we might say that utility is the power direct or indirect of producing pleasure or preventing pain. Or – the definition of the French writer Say, "It" (utility) "is the power which things possess of serving man in any manner whatsoever."[3] Of course utility properly is an abstract term – a mere quality of things. Some French writers especially have abused the word and turned it into a concrete and called it utilities – meaning the use of commodities. But we shall take the word commodities in that sense: – commodity = a thing having utility. Again, utility ought to correspond to

* ? (H. R.)
[3] Say, *Traité d'Economie Politique* (1819) tome ii, p. 506. Cf. *T.P.E.*, p. 38.

usefulness – or as Johnson says in his dictionary "usefulness [*blank in manuscript*]"[4] But in suggesting the term usefulness we must guard ourselves against any ambiguity, because usefulness is distinguished in common life from any refined or fancy pleasure. There is a distinction between fancy articles and useful articles and the same distinction runs thro' a good many other things. Nobody would say that fireworks were useful [? except][5] to the person who sells them. A diamond ring is not a useful article, so that useful is distinguished from ornamental or beautiful or fanciful. But then utility is not so restricted. Utility is the quality of anything in respect of its being desired or being wanted for any purpose whatsover – it may be even a ridiculous purpose. The tools of the housebreaker are objects of utility and would probably fetch a good price. So with dice or cards. Therefore in using the word utility we pay no respect to moral distinctions.

First. Utility is not an inherent property of things, because if so things are useful wherever they may be. Say, for instance that iron is useful, and nothing is really more useful, but does that mean that all iron is useful? Take again, the case of limestone or granite. These are useful, but then it does not mean that all granite is useful, because the quantity existing in mountains is millions of times as much as you can use in pavements. If the utility was inherent in things all pieces of granite ought to be as useful as that put down in our streets, all iron as useful as that in our pots and pans; coal in a mine before got out, as useful as that which is got out! So utility does not arise until the thing is brought into contact with the person wanting it. In short, utility is a relation between a thing wanted and the person wanting – and the one side of the relation is just as requisite as the other. I propose to call the physical qualities of thing whereby it becomes useful, potential utility; that is to say coal in a mine is potential utility, that is it might become useful under proper circumstances.

But potential utility has no place in political economy. We have nothing to do with it. It is more a question of chemistry as to what is coal and what is not coal and what might be used as fuel. But it really does not come into our view until it either is used or is cooked upon or going to be used – prospective utility.

Then there are some other definitions of utility that have been employed by French writers. Then Say, the best of the French economists, distinguishes between mediate and immediate utility.[6] Immediate utility – attaching to those things that can actually be consumed by a person: whereas mediate utility attaches to things that can be mediately

---

[4] The definition of utility given by Samuel Johnson was 'usefulness; profit; convenience; advantageousness' – *Dictionary of the English Language* (1822 ed.) p. 879.

[5] '? except' added in the margin of the manuscript, apparently by Rylett.

[6] Say, *Traité d'Economie Politique*, tome ii, p. 507.

exchanged. Money in a bank is of no use until you purchase something else with it, and you see that that distinction is somewhat different from the one already given – direct or indirect – the distinction of the chair used and the tools for making the chair.

Now the problem of political economy may be defined in this way, as the problem of maximising utility; or in other words supplying our wants to the highest possible point; but we must take into account the means of thus supplying ourselves which is by some kind of painful exertion. The object of utility means labour. Labour is thus the purchase price of utility – as it were. And the problem of political economy again is to obtain the most riches at the price of the least labour. Exactly the same idea is conveyed in the phrase of Prof. Hearne [sic]. He describes political economy as the theory of efforts to supply human wants:[7] and I may say that that, I believe, is derived almost verbally from a French writer whom I shall also have to mention occasionally – so you may as well know his name – Courcelle-Seneuille [sic].[8]

Now, there will naturally be two important divisions of the science of political economy. Naturally, we should first consider *what we want*, and then we should consider how we are to get what we want, or to use technical terms, there will be the consumption of wealth first, and secondly the production of wealth. These two parts have been very unequally considered by P. Economists; in fact some of them have professedly avoided the subject of consumption. In fact, I think none of the definitions I gave you mention the consumption of wealth. And then, again, Mill distinctly disclaimed any intention to treat the consumption of wealth. In his essays on some unsettled questions of political economy he says P.E. has nothing to do with the consumption of wealth further than as the consideration of it is inseparable from that of production, or from that of distribution. "We know not of any laws of the consumption of wealth as a subject of a distinct science. They can be no other than the laws of human enjoyment."[9] There may be some truth in what he says. I know no science of the laws of consumption, but then there is all the more reason that we should treat of them in the science of political economy. And a little thought will show you that it is indispensable. A manufacturer always thinks what he will produce – as to whether people will buy

[7] William Edward Hearn (1826–88), *Plutology: or the Theory of the Efforts to Satisfy Human Wants* (1864) pp. 6–7. Hearn was Professor of Greek in Queen's College, Galway, 1849–54, and Professor of Political Economy in the University of Melbourne from 1854: cf. D. B. Copland, *W. E. Hearn: First Australian Economist* (Melbourne, 1935).

[8] Jean-Gustave Courcelle-Seneuil (1813–98), *Traité Théorique et Pratique de l'Economie Politique*, 2 vols (1858–9; second edition 1867) I, 25, as quoted in *T.P.E.*, first edition, p. 49. Cf. Vol. IV, Letter 387, p. 59.

[9] 'Essays on Some Unsettled Questions of Political Economy' (1844) On the Definition of Political Economy', *Collected Works of John Stuart Mill*, vol. IV, *Essays on Economics and Society*, edited by J. M. Robson (Toronto, 1967) p. 318 (note).

what he is making. Therefore I agree much more with an earlier writer– the Earl of Lauderdale–who says that a great and important step in ascertaining the direction of industry seems to be the discovery of what dictates the proportion of demand for the various articles which are produced.[10] Then it comes practically to this, that we must first of all study the laws of human want so far as they are discoverable. This is distinctly Senior's opinion and he has very well spoken on it, and he lays down what he calls a law of variety in human wants, which contains, I believe, the true view of the subject. This is to the effect that our demand for any one kind of commodity is very limited in amount. That is to say that as soon as we are supplied with a certain amount of bread, from one to two pounds of bread per day, we cease to want any more bread. Therefore we begin to demand some more stimulating kind of food, say butter, then flesh, or eggs, or milk and so on. But after all your demand for food is limited and then you begin to think of your clothes, which you want as well as food. What is the limit to this? Well, one suit sometimes is sufficient. But then you want more, and then comes variety – dress suit, tourist suit, and so on – continual variety. The same with books. Variety is especially marked in books – scarcely want two copies of one book. Same principles may be seen acting in almost any case. Say a garden. You want more garden, but you would not make the second garden like the first. Certainly you would never have a series of gardens all the same – you would lay out different parts differently. So that this law of variety as laid down by Senior is undoubtedly true.

> Read very carefully beginning part of Senior. Begin at page 6 & go on to page 13.[11]

LECTURE III

THEORY OF UTILITY; PRODUCTION

Friday Oct. 22/75.

Now, we take P.E. as the theory of utility, or the theory of efforts to supply human wants. But there is one very important law as regards the origin of utility and that is what has been called the law of subordination of wants.

---

[10] James Maitland, eighth Earl of Lauderdale (1759–1839), *An Inquiry into the Nature and Origin of Public Wealth* (1804; second edition 1819), edited by Morton Paglin (New York, 1962) pp. 105–10.

[11] Senior, op. cit., containing chapter I, §1, 'Constituents of Wealth', with sub-sections on 'Utility', 'Limitation in Supply', 'Transferableness' and 'Limitation in Supply the most important', the last of which contains a statement of what Jevons terms Senior's 'law of variety' (pp. 11–12).

Any man may be considered to be a series of requirements felt with greater or less acuteness. They begin with the necessary and end with what we call the luxurious or simply ornamental. This point has been exceedingly well treated by Banfield,[1] whose work is called lectures on the organisation of labour – he has written very little on the subject of P.E. He observes that the lower wants man experiences in common with the Brutes: the mere craving of thirst and hunger, effects of heat and cold. Experience shows, however, that privations of various kinds affect men differently in degree according to the circumstances in which they are placed. Some feel the privations of certain employments, not so felt by others. Some sacrifice all that others hold dear, for the gratification of longings that are incomprehensible to their neighbours. Then he makes this remark: "Upon the complex foundation of lower wants and higher aspirations, the P. Est. has to build the theory of production and consumption."[2] In fact, he holds that this gives P.E. a scientific basis. And the first proposition of the theory of consumption is this: that the satisfaction of every lower want in the scale creates a desire of a higher character. This is perfectly accurate when by "creating" we mean that it allows the development of a desire of a higher character. It does not follow that everybody whose lower wants are satisfied will immediately acquire higher wants. That does not occur in the lower classes of mankind. In the tropics there are many plants that supply so much food that very little labour is required. It is said that one bread fruit tree will support a whole family. Cocoa-nuts, rice, maize and many other things afford sufficient food with very great ease in some parts of the world. Then it does not immediately follow that this class of mankind will immediately develop the fullness of civilisation. But it is quite true that we must have the lower wants satisfied before we can devote our attention to the higher ones. Accordingly, as Banfield says, the removal of a primary want commonly arouses the sense of more than one secondary privation.[3] A full supply of ordinary food not only excites to delicacy of eating but awakens attention to clothing, and the highest grade in the scale of wants, that of pleasure derived from beauties of nature and art. In this way it is that the consumption of objects of refined enjoyment has its lever in the facility with which the primary wants are satisfied. He looks upon this, quite truly I believe, as the key to the theory of value.

Now we may illustrate this in various ways. For instance, we may draw

---

[1] Thomas Charles Banfield, *Four Lectures on the Organization of Industry; being part of a course delivered in the University of Cambridge in Easter term 1844* . . . (1845). It has not proved possible to trace any definite biographical information concerning Banfield, an Englishman who travelled in Holland, Belgium and Germany during the 1840s and whose *Industry of the Rhine*, 2 vols (1846–8), is an important source of information on the early stages of industrialisation in Europe.

[2] Banfield, op. cit., p. 11.

[3] Ibid.

some important conclusions from it in a practical point of view. In a year when corn is dear, what will be the effect on the demand for other things? It is this, that as corn is the most necessary of all articles of food, therefore other things are sacrificed to corn. Therefore, those classes whose expenditure is to a large extent upon simple food will have less to expend upon other articles of enjoyment. But it would not be quite correct to say objects of luxury, for this reason that people who use very luxurious articles are not affected by the price of corn. The quantity of corn they eat, that is individually, is so little, and the price is so small a part of their income, that they don't feel it. But it does affect the luxuries of the poorer classes, which consist mainly of articles of clothing or bits of ornament. Accordingly a bad harvest is bad for the cotton trade because it restricts the consumption of cotton goods. That, again, is most particularly felt in the case of the demand from India because the immense population of India chiefly lives upon rice and to a great extent upon the merest necessaries of life, together with simple articles of clothing. Now, when the price of rice is high in India the demand for cotton goods is known to fall off very much.

This theory again is applied very satisfactorily to the corn laws in England. It has an important application as indicating that cheap corn would really be the best thing for farmers. That seems a paradox and probably no farmer would believe it, but Banfield pointed it out and it has come true simply in this way, that cheap corn allows of a large well fed (with corn) population and corn being cheap and they earning pretty good wages have a surplus which they will immediately proceed to expend in the next want.[4] Now doubtless that is partly in cotton goods and other manufactured articles; but then it also goes partly into better kinds of food. Then there is a large part of the land of the country which is very well suited for producing dairy produce and butchers meat, but is not very well suited for producing corn. Moreover arable industry and stock breeding help each other, the manure of the one promoting the production of corn by the other. As a matter of fact we know that all kinds of animal produce in this Kingdom are very remunerative to the farmers, all arising from the increase of population allowed by the free importation of corn.[5]

Then in very bad times we have the reverse effect and it is positively stated by Prof. Newman that in 1842 in Manchester no shops but *rag**

[4] Banfield, op. cit., p. 24.
[5] Modern authorities do not attribute any significant role in the nineteenth century population increase to the repeal of the Corn Laws. For detailed examination of the 'population revolution', see P. Deane and W. A. Cole, *British Economic Growth, 1688–1959* (Cambridge, 1969), and N. L. Tranter, *Population Since the Industrial Revolution* (1973).
* rock or rag. (H. R.)

shops could keep up their prices[6] – that was perhaps the last year in the history of the country in which there was really serious distress amounting to anything like a famine. It was much worse than in 1848.[7]

Now when we compare difft. commodities together in this way we shall find that they have as it were different laws of the variation of utility. That is to say the intensity of the desire for more is very variable; when the supply of corn falls off the price rises somewhat as the inverse square. Pp. 149, 154, of "Theory"[8] you find a statement of the manner in which the variation of the supply of corn causes the fluctuation in price, and the conclusions I come to are that it varies in the following way, that

$$\frac{5}{6(x-\frac{1}{8})^2}$$

(x being the harvest) represents the price of corn. What we want to make P.E. an exact science is the exact relation between the supply and the quantity (or the exact nature and formation of these curves.) This we may represent by curves

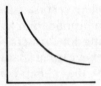

Sugar very much contrasts with corn because there are people who will take a great quantity of it if they can get it at a moderate price: but it is very expensive according to its nutritive contents, 3 or 4 times as much as bread. But we have no strong appetite for it and accordingly this is found to be the case, that a falling off in the supply of sugar does not raise its price much. This curve expresses its utility.

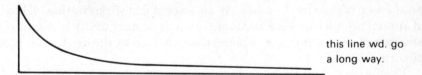

this line wd. go a long way.

---

[6] Francis William Newman (1805–97) *Lectures on Political Economy* (1851) p. 87. Newman, a Fellow of Balliol College, Oxford, 1826–30, Professor of Classical Literature, Manchester New College, 1840–6 and Professor of Latin, University College London, 1846–63, was a prolific writer on numerous subjects. He delivered a series of thirteen lectures on political economy at the Ladies' College, Bedford Square, and in the fourth, on 'Laws of Price', examined Banfield's assertion regarding the scale of human wants (see above, p. 14).

[7] On the severity of the depression of 1841–42 see R. C. O. Matthews, *A Study in Trade Cycle History: Economic Fluctuations in Great Britain, 1833–42* (Cambridge, 1954), especially pp. 214–17.

[8] *T.P.E.*, first edition.

If we could say that of so many millions of quarters of corn the price would be so much exactly, and when it fell off by that amount, that then the price would be so much and always would be under similar circs., then we should have an accurate mathematical law and we should be able to calculate the price of commodities under various circs. the one great obstacle is the fact that one substance is used so much in place of another. Potatoes cheap have somewhat the same effect as cheap corn or cheap rice, and I believe that one cause making the people comfortable at present is that potatoes are very cheap. But the difficulty is this, that potatoes take the place of corn, or oats the place of wheat, so that we are never able to get a definite quantity of one commodity as satisfying one particular want.

Production of wealth.—

Now, I propose to go on to production of wealth. We shall return to utility after a bit. The two sides of political E. are consumption and production, and I really don't know that it matters much which we take but the principles regarding the production of wealth are of a totally different nature from those regarding its consumption. To produce is to draw forth – the Product is that drawn forth. Accurately speaking production ought to be the act of drawing forth, but it is very ambiguous, and we now use it as the products of the country. But nothing can be more accurately descriptive than drawing forth and thus production is the accurate word – for this reason, that product is a portion of matter which is drawn forth and appropriated to our uses. We never create or destroy matter; therefore all that is done consists in moving substances and objects and putting them into their right places. I think it was Lord Palmerston who defined dirt as matter in the wrong place [9] – but then dirt is not always in the wrong place. But, then, I should say that wealth is matter in the right place. Then it follows that we want two principal things in production; and these are the requisites of production.   1. Labour.   2. Appropriate natural agents and objects. These are each of them absolutely necessary. It seems difficult to imagine that we can have utility without them. P.E.'s appear to take the person as representing labour. All beyond as representing agents or objects. Labour is characterised as simply the exertion of muscular force whereby we move things to and fro. (It is just conceivable that we might make use of other qualities of the body – e.g. a mother keeps her baby warm by the warmth of her own body.)* So labour simply resolves itself into action governed by the nervous action of the brain: so that one might say that labour is muscular action governed by intelligence. So kinds of mechanics require half and half mental and

[9] The Oxford English Dictionary, in describing this saying as 'modern' does not attribute it to Lord Palmerston.

* passages in brackets were "thrown in" as it were. (H. R.)

muscular labour: then comes the most purely intellectual labour. Does all exertion of the mind and body constitute labour in the economic sense? No, for this reason, that we undertake some of it for the immediate pleasure of the moment, without any ulterior object – various kinds of sports or a constitutional walk: but many not undertaken with any ulterior object therefore it would be of no use counting that as having pecuniary value.

Labour is any painful effort of body or mind directed to the acquisition of future good. The question of the real definition has never been solved. It is possible to object to this. But it is the definition I have always given. It is in Chap.v of the *Theory*.[10] But I will give you the definition of Say "Continued action directed towards an end".[11] But then that does not seem in the least to exclude a great many things. The use of the word painful is probably suggested by what Hearn says, namely, that the effort as the term seems to imply is more or less troublesome.[12] Practically we need never look to labour when it is a pleasure, but only when it is painful. It is a question whether labour or natural agents are more necessary to production and Mill says there is no question of comparison because both are *absolutely necessary*.[13] It is like asking which blade of a pair of scissors is most requisite for cutting whereas you actually cut with one against the other. The same with regard to an anvil and a hammer; or a Bank note – which half?

Read Ch.v of the Theory. Mill on Requisites of Production and Labour as an agent of Production – first two chaps. of 1st Book.

Write a brief essay on "What is the best definition of labour in an economic sense?" How you give some present inconvenience for a future good, and also in a shape that will realise pecuniary or other result – not including the work of animals.

---

[10] This passage almost paraphrases the definition given in *T.P.E.*, first edition, p. 164.

[11] 'Action suivie, dirigée vers un but' – Say, *Traité d'Economie Politique* (1819) tome ii, p. 506; cited by Jevons in *Principles of Economics*, p. 72.

[12] Hearn, *Plutology*, p. 24.

[13] Mill, *Principles*, book I, ch. I, § 4, pp. 29–30. The scissors analogy cited by Jevons is taken directly from Mill. Modern readers will be better acquainted with its use in the different context of demand and supply analysis by Marshall – *Principles of Economics*, book v, ch. III, § 7 (ninth edition, p. 348). If Marshall derived the analogy from Mill he did not acknowledge the fact.

LECTURE IV

PRODUCTION

Friday Oct. 29/75.

The main direction of labour. The great merit of Adam Smith is that he first insisted upon labour as the principal element in P.E. and the production of wealth. His work opens with a definition of labour.[1] He passes over altogether the branch of consumption, utility and those considerations we have had hitherto and starts with a definition. He says that "labour was the first price, the original purchase money, that was paid for all things. It was not by gold or silver but by labour that all the wealth of the world was originally purchased."[2] It is true that John Locke had nearly a century before pointed out that the activity of labour seemed to be the cause of wealth rather than the material resources of the countries as we should call them now.[3] The very richest countries such as Mexico have a wretchedly poor population if the population is inactive. So that the whole rests in fact upon labour, or as it is expressed in several proverbs "The gods sell all to labour". It might be worth considering how far labour is an actual requisite even of enjoyment itself. We have already partially discussed the matter, but according to Sir Wm. Hamilton pleasure is the reflex of perfect or successful energy,[4] and I supply the word successful as an explanation of perfect. So that it is quite a question how far labour in itself is an element in . . . [*pleasure*]* provided that it is moderate in amount and also has that success of bringing the expected result. In fact whether it will or will not be pleasureable depends on whether it does or does not appear - - - - - - - - † to the intended end. On the one hand nothing is more painful than labour without result and the worst punishment that has been devised is useless labour – treadmill. And it is perfectly well known that of all forced labour that of slaves or convicts is exceedingly inefficient because it is unaccompanied by any motive to exertion and is therefore given in the worst possible way.

One very important point to remark about labour is this, that the painfulness of it varies according to duration and rises the longer it is

[1] Adam Smith (1723–90), *An Inquiry into the Nature and Causes of the Wealth of Nations* (1776) I, 1. Page references are to the edition by Edwin Cannan, 2 vols (1904).

[2] Smith, *Wealth of Nations*, book I, chapter v; I, 32–3.

[3] John Locke (1632–1704), 'Essay concerning the true original extent and end of civil government' (1689) book II, chapter v, §§ 40–4, *The Works of John Locke*, 10 vols (1823) v, 361–4.

[4] J. S. Mill, *An Examination of Sir William Hamilton's Philosophy* . . ., third edition (1867) p. 540: 'Pleasure is a reflex of the spontaneous and unimpeded exertion of a power, of whose energy we are conscious.'

* word lost. (H. R.)

† ? necessary. (H. R.)

continued. That is a point that has been little considered by P. Economists, but it is really one of the elementary points of the subject. When we speak of long continued labour we mean in proportion to the 24 hours. Of course men are periodic in their habits – arising from the revolution of the earth – so that the 24 hours is as it were the scope – the period which alone we need consider in measuring labour. A man in his normal state does not work all night except in special emergencies. No man can go on for more than a day or two. So that we have alternate periods of labour and rest; then we have to consider what fraction of the 24 hours may be considered a moderate amount of labour. There are men who work 16 hours to 20 hours during a portion of the year – which is more than a man can do for any length of time – 16 hours is perhaps the limit. But the great principle is this – that as you extend the time of labour the painfulness and injury done to the frame increases very rapidly. We might represent it in this way.

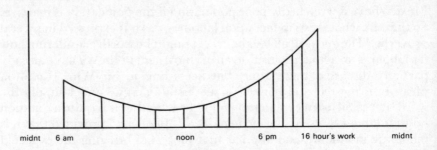

If we take 6 a.m. as the time for beginning I should be inclined to represent the painfulness of *labour** as being considerable just at the beginning. A man beginning always feels it irksome, especially beginning at 6 o'clock in the morning. When once you have begun your work it becomes more easy. You get your hand in. That I would represent by the falling of the line. Then during a considerable portion of the day the labour is rather agreeable than otherwise but it is towards the latter part of the day that a person becomes tired. So with reading a book – it is wearisome at first. Then we get very much excited, and later on it becomes wearisome again. So it is very bad to read one book more than one or two hours. The length of the line represents the intensity of the painfulness. That is a very important consideration, because it shows how much better it is if one or two hours can be knocked off a day's work,

* ? does not this mean "exertion" because suppose a man walks some distance to his work, has he not shaken off dull sloth by the time he handles his tools!   (H. R.)

within moderate limits. Sixteen hours work will be exceedingly painful, but 12 hours not very painful. Eight hours would not be painful.

Then one result we are to draw from this is that if you get down to a moderate number of hours there would be harm in reducing it further: or if you get down to ten hours we don't save very much pain as it were in knocking off two hours, but when we get down to eight, it would be absurd to go lower having regard to the laws of production.

We will go on to consider the mode in which labour is applied in Mill's second chapter on Labour as an agent of production.[5] You find a kind of enumeration of five indirect modes of applying labour. Labour may be directly applied to the satisfaction of wants – domestic servants – that of the coachman who drives you, or your men who in India or China carry you. That would be direct I suppose. But the five modes of indirect application are as follows: 1st. Extractive Industry; Labour employed in producing any = drawing forth = materials upon which industry is afterwards to be employed. In many cases this is a labour of mere appropriation – merely the labour of putting out your hands and taking the thing. It begins with the gathering of wild fruits – capturing wild animals. But of course we remember that, because you don't labour to produce these things, it does not follow that we get them easily. The labour of gathering some kinds of fruit spread over a large surface – such as forestry – may be great. Then it includes also such things as work in a mine, cutting timber, and finally all agriculture including raising of cotton, silk, flax, and so on.

II.   Labour employed in making tools, implements, machines and other necessary aids for the assistance of future labour. These tools and machines are of all kinds and sizes, from a flint and steel to a steamship.

III.   Labour employed in the production of Industry and in providing buildings, warehouses, docks, granaries, etc.

IV.   Labour employed in carrying distributing the products of other labour.

V.   Education.

VI.   The labour of invention.

I won't dwell on these because in the first place you have them in Mill's second chapter,[6] and you get fully from him all that needs to be said, and secondly because I don't think it of very much importance – except as directing attention to the various ways labour is employed, but there is no *proven** difference between labour. It includes all from mere gathering to the well cultivated form. It would be impossible to distinguish between II and III; because there is no especial difference between the making of

[5] Mill, *Principles*, book i, chapter ii, pp. 35–40.
[6] Mill, *Principles*, pp. 35–44.
*   ?   (H. R.)

tools and the making of buildings requisite for the purpose. A dock is as much a machine as a ship. The one moves and the other does not, that is all. Again we are told that the making of hedges and fences would be labour employed in production, whereas the rest of agricultural labour is of the first class; but the making of hedges is just as agricultural as any of the others. The definitions then are not very important tho' I expect you to be acquainted with them.

We will consider now how it is that labour may be employed with greatest advantage; and there are several ways of putting it. We might put it in this way: Labour must be employed

    1st At the time
    2nd At the place
    3rd in the manner

in which the product shall bear the greatest proportion to the amount of labour. That is perhaps the most comprehensive statement of what is involved in economical production. We shall have to consider various devices for increasing production which will have to come under one or other of these heads. E.g. Capital comes under the first as to time. The question of foreign trade and what we call perpetual division of labour comes under the second, of raising things in the place where the soil is most fertile for them or the circs. suitable.

Just for the present we will consider the third head, the manner of employing labour, and that we may divide under two heads:

I. The skill or knowledge with which labour is directed.

II. Assistance derived from the division of labour, including all methods of cooperation or combination of labour.

Then comes the question of skill and knowledge. The fact is that our whole power arises from our knowledge. Bacon says "Knowledge is power". In his muscular construction a man is not superior to many animals and is vastly inferior to a lion or tiger. A horse is far more strong – equal to five or seven men. We get rule simply because we have logical intellect and are able to see the effects of what we do. Bacon says "Knowledge is power because ignorance of a cause loses us the effect. We can rule nature only by obeying her, and what we established as a course by contemplation becomes a rule in operation". That is the third aphorism of Bacon's Novum Organon [sic] [7] and is exceedingly well worth study because it contains the whole gist and point of the use of knowledge. The same idea no doubt was expressed long ago by Virgil in a celebrated line

  Felix etc.   "Happy is he who knows
         the causes of things."[8]

---

[7] Jevons appears to have based his translation of the third Aphorism on the version appearing in

or it was expressed still better in recent times by Johnson who put it very aptly in 5 words

"Ruling by obeying natures powers." [9]

Now you will easily see that this remark of Bacon is perfectly correct because in order to bring a certain thing about, we must know the cause or condition under which it can be brought about and with a proper amount of knowledge we can indefinitely avail ourselves of nature. One of the simplest illustrations of this is the case of rowing upon a river or tidal sea. A man void of intelligence might row, but he would row against the tides, but a man of intelligence observes that the tide is in his favour and the consequence is that he avails himself of the motion of the tides. In rowing upon a rapid river an experienced boatman knows which side to keep as to the current.

In former days there was very little knowledge of the character of the winds in any particular part except as to trade winds; but by a system of observation started by - - - - - - - - - - -* [10] charts have been constructed showing the probable prevalence of the winds in almost every part of the ocean that is traversed. Thus that is the most intelligent way of availing ourselves of the winds to the best effect because the captain then chooses out his road just in those tracks of the ocean where the winds are favourable to him in that season of the year; and avoids the other tracks. If navigation by sailing ships were likely to be the prevailing mode of navigation that would be a most important matter, but then we know it is superseded by steam navigation and captains don't think very much about winds except as producing disagreeable waves. But even steam is only a better way of taking advantage of the powers of nature – of knowing what causes will produce motion.

It is also worth while to consider the 4th aphorism of Bacon. "Man in his works can do nothing more than move things towards or from each

---

The Physical and Metaphysical Works of Lord Bacon, including his . . . Novum Organum, edited by J. Devey (1860) p. 383.

[8] Publius Vergilius Maro (70–19 B.C.), *Georgics*, ii, 490, 'Felix qui potuit rerum cognoscere causas'.

[9] Rylett evidently misheard this: the quotation 'And ruling by obeying Nature's powers' is line 40 of Tennyson's *Ode sung at the Opening of the International Exhibition*. See A. E. Baker, *Concordance to the Poetical and Dramatic Works of Alfred, Lord Tennyson* (1914) p. 595.

* ? (H. R.)

[10] Probably Matthew Fontaine Maury (1806–73), officer in the United States Navy; Professor of Physics at the Virginia Military Institute from 1868 until his death. His main interest lay in promoting maritime commerce and sail technology by improving navigational techniques; devised charts of the general circulation of atmosphere and ocean based on data on winds and currents contained in ships' logs, published as *Wind and Current Charts*, beginning with the North Atlantic in 1847; also author of *Physical Geography of the Sea* (1855). Cf. Rear-Admiral R. Fitzroy, *The Weather Book: a manual of Practical Meteorology* (1863) pp. 48–54.

other. Nature working with him accomplishes the rest."[11] Now this partly expresses the idea you find in Mill's chapter that men only move things. "Labour in the physical world is always - - - - - - - - - - - in putting things in motion.[12] The laws of nature do the rest"[13] and that contains the same as Bacon's 4th aphorism.

But we may nevertheless discriminate two distinct kinds of change which we effect in natural objects. The first is what we may call molar or mechanical change – or we may call it the production of visible motion. Prof. Stewart speaks of visible energy or rather visible motion:[14] i.e. when you move an object of visible or appreciable size. That we distinguish from molecular or chemical change where the change is in the atoms of the subjects. We see no motion, but only observe a change in the character of the substance.

Now, there is some difference between these two, because in the case of molar change the economy of labour is effected by substituting the energy of natural objects for our muscular energy; and the change is of a kind that we can accomplish by our own energy. In fact in very unadvanced communities the whole of this work may be said to be done by hand. In some of the unprogressed mountain tribes all conveyance of goods is done by carrying: corn is ground by stones: agriculture is carried on by rudest tools. The greatest progress that has been made in civilisation consists in the substituting the powers of animal labour for conveyance. Water power (including tidal water):— very unprogressive peoples employ rude kinds of water mills. Next we came to use wind and subsequently steam. Sir John Hershell [sic] has given a very interesting statement of four different ways in which knowledge assists us.[15]

I.   In showing us how to avoid attempting impossibilities. He remarks that a great many proposals have been made which are impracticable – such as perpetual motion; navigating balloons; using electricity as a prime mover. I believe that is an impossibility. Deliberate scientific consideration of some of these would show that these are impossibilities.

II.   In securing us from mistakes in attempting possible objects by inadequate or unsuitable means. In some cases, he observes, people had

---

[11] Cf. Works of Lord Bacon, p. 383.

[12] Rylett added a note in the margin here, which appears to read: '? unable to verify this and many others because a portion of my best books lost in transit'. He made several moves up and down the country, and to Ireland, in the course of his career as a Unitarian minister. See Vol. V, Letter 605, n. 1, p. 54.

[13] 'Labour, then, in the physical world, is always and solely employed in putting objects in motion; the properties, of matter, the laws of nature, do the rest,' Principles, book 1, chapter 1, § 2, p. 28.

[14] Almost certainly Balfour Stewart, Professor of Natural Philosophy at Owens College, Manchester, at that period. See Vol. III, Letter 333, n. 2, p. 236.

[15] Sir John F. W. Herschel, A Preliminary Discourse on the Study of Natural Philosophy (1831; new edition 1851) p. 44. See Vol. II, p. 432, n. 1.

actually laboured to produce a result by the very mode that was the least likely to produce it – of which perhaps the best instance is that of making iron in a blast furnace. It used to be thought that to make good iron the blast ought to be cold. But eventually it was found out that if you heated it it was much better.

III.   In enabling us to accomplish in the easiest shortest and most economical and most effectual manner. A comprehensive head, this, including the use of machinery.

IV.   Science induces us to attempt and enables us to accomplish objects which but for such knowledge we should never have thought of undertaking. Instance: electric telegraph. It was hardly possible to conceive such a thing, much less to believe it would be really carried out before the powers of electricity were shown.

In conjunction with this subject it is well to note the manner in which we may classify machines in a definite way. Stated by Mr. Babbage in his Economy of Manufactures[16] that machines – not necessarily the whole of the machine but the parts of it which have a distinct purpose – may be classified in this way.

1.   Those which produce power, that is prime movers. By producing power we only mean that they *appropriate** for us some of the energy of inferior nature – this includes horse power, water mills, wind mills, tidal mills, steam engines etc. of all kinds.

2.   Averaging machines – those which accumulate and average power. They are of considerable importance, – illustrate this chiefly by the fly wheel. Power is a thing that can be poured in or out as you can pour liquid in or out of a jug. When you get a wheel into motion you put power into it and when you stop it, you get it out, and then in many machines the power has to be exerted momentarily or at remote intervals *or for the short time - - - - - - - - - -*. It is an advantage then to take a great wheel in which you can accumulate power between the motions. That is particularly noticeable in rolling mills – which would be stopped but for the fly wheel.

Then in later times there are the hydraulic accumulation machines – much used now in Armstrong's apparatus.[17] As men pour water continuously into an accumulator they are able to exert great

[16] Charles Babbage, *On the Economy of Machinery and Manufactures* (1832). Babbage (1792–1871) was Lucasian Professor of Mathematics in the University of Cambridge, 1828–39, and one of the principal founders of the Royal Statistical Society; devoted the greater part of his life and fortune to the development of a calculating machine. The passages referred to here occur on pp. 16–28 of the fourth edition (1835).

*   ? (H. R.)
*   ? "or for a short time e.g. wind." (H. R.)
[17] The hydraulic crane invented in 1846 by Sir William Armstrong. See Vol. IV, Letter 438, p. 127.

power at any moment that they choose, as in the opening of dock gates. This produces great economy of power because a man working one or two hours can accomplish as much work as six men called together for the purpose.

3.   Regulating machines which are best represented by the governor of the steam engine which keeps the engine in equal motion under great difficulties of work, and the regulating apparatus has been brought to considerable perfection in late years.

4.   There is another device called extracting in Cornish engines. Those which increase the intensity or increase or diminish the velocity. It includes a great many machines even from such a simple thing as a crowbar which diminishes the velocity of action.

5.   There are a few cases which extend the action of force over a long period of time – reverse of the last, and best represented by winding up a clock – which consists in putting a considerable amount of energy into a clock in the short time occupied in winding up and then the clock goes on for 24 hours gradually expending itself.

Read Chapter on Productive and Unproductive labour in Mill.[18] Also begin reading the first chapter in Smith's Wealth of Nations – the Ch. on the division of labour.[19]

LECTURE V

DIVISION OF LABOUR

Nov. 5/75.

The means of increasing the production of such labour – that is in fact the main problem of P.E. We shall find ultimately that the wages, the receipts of the *far** largest classes of the *needy,* if not the whole indeed, depend upon the productiveness of labour. But we ought to attach a definite idea to the productiveness of labour. Of course other things being the same the larger quantity of any commodity yielded by a certain quantity of labour, the greater its productiveness. That seems self evident. But, on the other hand, you must remember that the utility of the commodity is not necessarily proportioned to its quantity. On the other hand, the irksomeness or pain of labour is, again, *not proportioned*† to its duration. So

---

[18]   Mill, *Principles,* book I, chapter III, 'Of Unproductive Labour', pp. 45–54.
[19]   Smith, *Wealth of Nations,* book I, chapter I; I, 5–14.
*   ? four   (H. R.)
†   ? in proportion   (H. R.)

that what we have really to compare is the utility produced as compared with the amount of pain undertaken. That is rather difficult. But making the proviso we may now look simply to the multiplication of the produce, which after all is the main source of increasing utility. And, as Adam Smith says, the greatest improvements in the productive powers of labour, and the greater part of the skill, dexterity, and judgment with which it is anywhere directed or applied seem to have been the effects of the division of labour. This subject of the division of labour is treated in the first three chapters.[1] He begins by taking the pin manufacture as a kind of introductory illustration, as showing the wonderful increase of product arising fr. the dividing of that work, only intending it as an illustration of the same division as extends throughout society. All industrious society is a great machine, as it were, with different parts appropriated to different kinds of work. And as each factory is a part only of the industry of the country, so each workman in a factory is a part of the machine in that factory, as it were = a sub-division. In fact, it would not be bad to speak of the division of labour as occurring between persons not in the same building – not in the same form as a subdivision in other circs.

I might just remark that one writer has objected to this expression "division of labour" altogether – that in place of a division of labour it is really a union of labour. Divided labour, in one sense, would consist in each person working apart from and independent of others – so that in the primitive state of industry there is the greatest division in that respect. But this is a division of a totally different meaning. It is the division of the total operation to be done. But that division necessitates the union of the labour of different persons. i.e. if one person made the *pin*,* another the point, and so on, then they must unite together to produce the pin. It is something analogous to extension and intension in logic. Wakefield is the writer and is worth attending to.[2] But I think if we understand what we talk about; if we understand the division of employments requires the union of labourers it cannot give rise to any difficulty and therefore we will continue the expression.

Then we come to Adam Smith's enumeration of the advantages of the division of labour.

[1] Smith, *Wealth of Nations*, book 1, chapters I–III; 1, 5–23.

* head   (H. R.)

[2] Jevons appears to have made considerable use in this lecture of the extended 'Note on Chapter 1, Book 1' in Edward Gibbon Wakefield's edition of the *Wealth of Nations*. In this Wakefield had argued that Smith's famous term 'division of labour' was misleading and should be replaced by 'division of employments'. '. . . the division of employments which takes place in a pin-factory, results from, and is wholly dependent on, the union, generally under one roof, of all the labour by which the pins are made. Though no entire pin be made by any one person, each pin is the produce of many persons' united labour' – [E. G. Wakefield] *An Inquiry into the Nature and Causes of the Wealth of Nations by Adam Smith, LL.D., with a commentary by the author of 'England and America'* (1840) vol. 1, p. 25. Cf. below, Lecture VI, pp. 34–5.

I. Increase of dexterity arising from every particular workman being occupied in one kind of work only, to which he becomes perfectly adapted, e.g. nail making: watch-making: engraving: dexterity of a good accountant.

II.   Saving of time commonly lost in passing from one species of work to another. Smith thinks a man saunters when changing his occupations. There is a certain difficulty to adapt ourselves to new work, so that those who do different kinds of work in a day become rather slothful in consequence. There is considerable truth in this, but it is not very important. Yet in another sense it is. There are many operations which demand a succession of acts with a variety of tools or other arrangements. Now, if the same workman has to change his tools very frequently there is great loss of time – in fact that is the principal cause of loss of time in nail making by hand because a man in making a nail has to put down his hammer, blow the bellows of the fire, take the rod out of the fire, then hammer the point of the nail, then make another operation for the head of the nail. Steel pens, a good instance. Therefore such things are made by passing quantities of them through one machine continually. The only question remaining concerning this is as to whether the change of occupation is not advantageous in many cases, as to whether continually doing the same occupation about a pin or pen is not an excessively monotonous and injurious thing. Or the same with a clerk. You would think the change advantageous economically. But it is difficult to find a case where it is so. Clearing House clerks, for instance, do the same thing continually. [3]

III.   The invention of a great number of machines which facilitated the abridged labour and enabled one man to do the work of many. Observe that it is not the use of machines that he is here referring to exactly. It is the invention of them: that is to say, the division of labour facilitates invention because a man by constantly having his thoughts upon one single occupation is more likely to discover improvements than if his thoughts were distracted by doing a great number of things. It seems to me this is a . . . . [4] mistake of Smith. It would amount to this: that the narrower a man's ideas are the more ingenious he is, and I believe experience does not bear that out in any adequate degree. A certain number of instances may be mentioned in which men have hit upon things in the way he mentions. On the other hand most great inventions have been made by men of great information and ability. The greatest inventors are men who invent many things like Boulton [5] and Watts [sic], [6]

---

[3] See Jevons, *Money and the Mechanism of Exchange* (1878) pp. 263–8.

[4] Gap in text.

[5] Matthew Boulton (1728–1809), founder of the Soho engineering works, Birmingham, in which Watt was his partner from 1775 to 1800; inventor of the steam coining presses in use in the Royal Mint until the late nineteenth century.

Stephenson,[7] Roberts,[8] Nasmyth,[9] Bessemer,[10] Siemens.[11] The first of English inventors was William Lee,[12] who invented the knitting machine. So the third head requires modification.

There are certain advantages laid down by Chas. Babbage, as for instance:[13]

IV. Multiplication of efficiency which arises when many things can be done at once with little more labour than a single thing. He is not referring to the repeating of the same operation exactly but to the one operation itself having a multiplied efficiency. It is illustrated by such things as procuring information. A great number of people want to know what the weather tomorrow will be; then if by an elaborate arrangement of telegraph posts you can acquire once for all a clear idea of the weather that is likely to be, and then inform a vast number of people, by that there is an enormous increase of efficiency. The same thing applies to almost all the information gathered by newspapers. One man may report a particular market (and send the report of it to every daily paper in the Kingdom). Something the same occurs in all govt. appointment arrangements, for instance the police *a divided case of labour* [a case of divided labour]. The inhabitants take it easy while a few men watch over them and the work is done most efficiently. But the best instance of all is the post office: for this reason: Because a postman is able to carry a great many letters at once almost as easily as a single letter; and, again, in the conveyance of the mails, if you have got a train running from Manchester to London you might as well have a few tons of letters as a few cwts. Therefore in almost all arrangements of the post office *the increase of labour is in no proportion to the increase of work done.* That is the source of the enormous net revenue of the post office.

V. The multiplication of efficiency from machine like repetition and the identity of the work done. This and some other advantages are described by Babbage in his Economy of Manufactures.[14] This involves most of the advantages of machinery, and it is obvious that when once

---

[6] James Watt (1736–1819), patented the steam engine in 1769 and developed it in partnership with Boulton.

[7] George Stephenson (1787–1848), railway pioneer; built 'The Rocket' in 1829.

[8] Richard Roberts (1789–1864), noted for his invention of an automatic mule during a cotton spinners' strike in 1825.

[9] James Nasmyth (1808–90), associated with the invention of the steam hammer. See Vol. II, Letter 62, n. 3, pp. 151–2.

[10] [Sir] Henry Bessemer (1813–98) invented the cheap, rapid process for steel manufacture which bears his name.

[11] Sir William Siemens (1823–83), inventor of the regenerative furnace, patented in 1856, which contributed to the massive increase in steel production made possible by the 'Bessemer process'.

[12] William Lee (d. 1610?), inventor of the stocking frame.

[13] Babbage, op. cit., pp. 30–9.

[14] Ibid., pp. 69–113.

you can get an arrangement which will perfect a particular kind of work you get an enormous economy. The best case is that of printing. In former ages every book had to be copied. Therefore the labour spent upon books or MSS. was proportioned to the number of them. A hundred copies = 100 men to write them [or what is equivalent to that] to say nothing of the mistakes. But with the printing press you spend a great deal of money in setting up types once for all. The same in the making of money. The more made, the cheaper, or in the case of books. The same with bank notes – only one original engraving. So that they never have a second original copy. In this way the case applies to any particular kind of work that can be done by routine. You see that the same thing operates in office work etc. – where you would expect it. All work you call routine work is distinguished by this, that it requires no thought or separate treatment. You establish a rule or precedent as to the way in which it has to be done, and in a well arranged office the thing has to be done almost like machinery.

One case of the multiplication of efficiency which I meant to mention was the Clearing House. It involves the multiplication of efficiency because when once you have a number of cheques drawn upon the same house, they may be all paid in one lump sum: you don't require to make a separate payment for each. You add them all up at once, and if the same house has to make a number of payments and a number of receipts the same day it balances the one against the other. So that the payment of millions of money is achieved by nothing but a certain amount of counting as it were. This partly depends upon repetition because the clearer receives a quantity of cheques and these are sorted out so as to come to him and are all added up together, and sent *home in his bag, so he treats them by routine and passes them by merely balancing amounts.**[15]

VI.   There is a further advantage – personal adaptation of the labourer to the work undertaken. Everybody must allow there are diffces. of formation in people; then if such diffces. in the physical frame why not in nervous organisation? And facts prove that there is a diffce. It is true that a century ago there was a great disinclination to believe the diffce. of organisation. It was said all diffces. were unfavourable circs. of birth. But the last 20 or 30 years have changed opinion on that point. Then if there are innate diffces. – I mean those which are caused by circs. incident to birth and education – if there are these diffces. of course it is desirable that for each man a suitable kind of work should be found. A man of delicate organisation should become a watch-maker; a man with powerful muscles is suitable for a blacksmith; a man with an arithmetical mind

* ? (H. R.)
[15] Jevons, *Money and the Mechanism of Exchange*, pp. 263–89.

might become an accountant. There are endless diffces. which no doubt tend to develop themselves by the progress of civilisation.

Smith discusses this question and thinks these diffces. are to a great extent created by occupation – that is in accordance with opinion today. Children, he thinks, are very much alike.¹⁶ I am far from denying that education does alter people immensely. The blacksmith does acquire strength. The character of the body does become suited to our work; but it does not follow that all these diffces. arise from birth.

Read Adam Smith's 1st 3 chaps. and all that Mill says on this subject up to the end of Chap. ix.

LECTURE VI

DIVISION OF LABOUR (continued)

Nov. 12/75.

VII. The advantages of local adaptation gives rise to the *territorial division of labour* – that is to say that kinds of industry tend to locate themselves in difft. parts either of one country or of one nation – in which case we call it inland trade – or between difft. countries =international trade and division of labour. The advantages thus derived are from two distinct sources, first from the material or external characteristics of the place, i.e. soil, climate, mineral wealth, etc., and 2nd. from the character of the people who happen to be upon that spot. It is quite obvious that any industry requiring coal must be set up in a coal district, or a water industry where water is abundant, and so with others of the sort. [We shall come to this again under the subject of natural agents.] And it is sufficiently obvious that there are many things which can only be produced in a particular climate – wine for instance. But then 2ndly the character of the people influences territorial division of labour because there are undoubtedly diffces. of races and civilisation and temperament and "people are the most difficult of all kinds of goods to remove".¹ The dislike to go amongst difft. manners and customs so great that some nations hardly ever move at all. The French, for instance, don't emigrate and so of other nations, tho' it is less true of the English people and Teutons, etc.

Then we have to observe this, that particular peoples in particular

---

¹⁶ Smith, *Wealth of Nations*, book I, chapter II; I, 17–18.

¹ '. . . it appears evidently from experience that a man is of all sorts of luggage the most difficult to be transported . . .', Smith, *Wealth of Nations*, book I, chapter VIII; I, 77.

places appear to acquire special aptitudes for kinds of work. Whether it is that knowledge is delivered like tradition, or whether it is actually in some degree innate is difficult to decide. Or again whether by long experience people learn the exact manner of carrying on any work. Case in point: difficulty of producing wines equal to those of France and Germany. Australia appears suited to the growth of wines and so does California and attempts have been made to grow wine, and people have been brought over from France and Germany and yet in Australia they can't produce the same perfection of flavour as in France. But perhaps they have not found the best spots. And then, I apprehend a kind of experience has been accumulated that can't be expected in a new country.

The same thing may be said about England, where trade is settled in different spots. Metals at B'ham, steel at Sheffield. It is not possible to give any explanation except that these trades have become hereditary in these difft. places, and the chief difficulty is to say whether it is traditional or innate.

This territorial division of labour does not exist merely between difft. parts of a country but also in towns. In London, for example, banking business in Lombard St. Lawyers, Lincoln's Inn and Temple. Newspaper business, Strand. Booksellers in Paternoster Row. Stockbrokers, exchange Corn dealers, Mark Lane. Tea and sugar, Mincing Lane. Watchmakers in Clerkenwell – which is a remarkable case and one of great antiquity – every part of a watch which a man makes is posted on his door.

This division of labour or localisation of industry is remarked in Hearne. [2] Also described in the Comp. Almanack for 1855, and even the districts in which the people live are marked. Coachmakers in . . . .* [3] Sugar refiners in Stepney and Whitechapel. Fishmen, Billingsgate. Silk weaving, Spitalfields. Tailors, St. James, Marylebone. The origin of these will be found to be in many cases historical accident, but when any cause gives rise to it it tends to perpetuate in consequence of proximity for ease of transporting parts of a watch.†

In some countries, division of labour between towns and ports is not so distinct in England as in Holland last century and the century before. Heidelberg, great seat of the wine trade. Shipbuilding in London. Lessing had East Indian trade.* [4]

    [2] Hearn, *Plutology*, pp. 305–7.
    *   ?   (H. R.)
    [3] 'Coachmakers in St. Pancras and Marylebone', *The British Almanac for . . . MDCCCLV . . . With 'The Companion to the Almanac; or year book of general information* . . ., p. 80, quoted in Hearn, op. cit., p. 305.
    † See Note A at end of section.   (H. R.)
    *   ? Notes imperfect here.   (H. R.)
    [4] Rylett evidently misheard this passage, based on Hearn, *Plutology*, p. 306: 'In Holland, during

But now, let us consider the actual form division of labour takes in any society. We find that it only takes a double form of division. A cross classification becomes necessary to express it. We must have a tabular form in which in one direction we have the class of industry and then in the other direction you will have the orders of industry.[5]

Classes of trade

Cotton, wool, silk, flax, iron, copper, timber.

Orders of Industry	retailers
	warehousemen
	1 manufacturers
	dealers in raw materials & producers of raw materials.
	proprietors of places where raw material is produced.

and one depends upon the *material work traded*† in; the other upon the operation done with that material as e.g. we have in classes of trade, cotton, wool, flax, iron, copper, timber and so on. These orders are not always distinctly separated: for instance: a vineyard proprietor is a distinct person, but very often he will work his own vineyard. However sometimes no doubt the vineyard will be worked by one and owned by another. Then, we have no *dealers** in raw materials exactly. But in Spain the wine is brought up in a rough state, taken to Cadiz and is there manufactured into what we call sherry:[6] then imported into England and the wholesale merchant would be represented here, and then there are plenty of retailers. In Cotton the proprietors are represented by the owners of the land in South America. The producers of raw materials, those who grow the cotton. The dealers would be the exporters, the merchants and brokers. Then the manufacturers are, of course, the friends in Manchester. But they are broken up into several difft. grades – for instance, spinner, he is to a certain extent a speculator; then weaver, then yarn merchant or dealer, who passes the spun cotton over to

---

the days of its commercial greatness, various branches of commerce selected as it were each some favourite town. Middleburg was the great seat of the wine trade. Flessing almost monopolized the East India trade. Shipbuilding was the chief business of Saardam . . .'

[5] The classification of trades was a subject to which Jevons always attached peculiar importance. Cf. *Principles of Economics*, chapter XXIII, which deals with this topic. On p. 107 of this chapter Jevons wrote: 'My own early studies of economics may be said to have commenced with this subject. Starting with Dr. Farr's system of statistics of the 1851 census, I made an elaborate investigation in the years 1856 and 1857 of the trade portion of the London Directory, and compiled statistics intended to be the foundation . . .' [The passage is incomplete.]

† ? (H. R.)

* ? (H. R.)

[6] The traditional centre of sherry manufacture is Jerez de la Frontera; Cadiz is the principal port of the region.

the weaver, then the agent or dealer in the grey cloth, who hands it over to the printer, then the finisher and other minor parts – he then leaves it in the hands of the warehouseman thro' whom it passes to the shops. The series not so complete in silk. But if there be two kinds of operations done by difft. people, then there will be an order of dealers arising between them – a dealer = a kind of middle man.

Corn trade: the proprietor = land owner, producer = farmer, corn dealer, miller, flour dealer, baker. But this does not give any idea of the complexity of difft. trades; only the main outline. But there are complicated inter connections and minor trades which don't run into this series at all, or are only incidentally connected with any of them. We might call subsidiary trades those which supply any of the implements or do simple operations connected with any more important trade. The cotton trade employs an immense number of subsidiary trades. Again, this appears extensively in the corn business. For example we find that bakers employ oven builders, which is a distinct trade; peddle makers; then the millers work employs at least half a dozen difft. trades. Millstones: two trades, importer, trader and cutter. Then millwrights. *Some machine* . . . .* used for separating the bran,[7] separate trade. Corn merchants employ 6 difft. trades: corn meter = for measuring corn. He employs the corn measure maker. In some places a definite trade, the granary owners and granary keepers. Farming = a great number of subsidiary trades. Farmers employ a number – seed dealers, trade in manure, bone dealers, agricultural implement makers, and then there are agricultural implement owners and there are agents, people who arrange for the purchase or hire of these machines.

Simple co-operation of Labour. According to Wakefield,[8] what we have hitherto considered is after all only one branch of the combination of labour, that branch in which difft. people labour in difft. occupations. In fact Wakefield objected to division of labour and substituted division of employment.[9] Curious that the more division of labour there is the more workmen are united together. The oven builder is connected with the baker, e.g. So that division of labour produces dependence and union of worker. Therefore I think Wakefield is right in speaking of division of employment. He divided labour into complex and simple. Complex = where they work together in difft. manners. Simple = where they work in the same manner. Simple = a number of men pulling at the same rope. One of the best instances = regiment of soldiers. All men in this

---

* Bolting?   (H. R.)
    [7] Bolting is the process by which meal is separated from chaff, and of which bran is a by-product. Jevons had presumably referred to a machine used for the purpose.
    [8] *Wealth of Nations*, ed. Wakefield (1840), 'Note on Chapter 1, Book 1'; 1, 297. Cf. above, p. 27.
    [9] Wakefield, loc. cit., 1, 26; cf. above, p. 27.

are working simply. But an officer's is a complex labour. On board ship two men at the same rope e.g. but many of the crew appointed to difft. tasks, engineer, carpenter, and so on. The officers of the ship are in complex co-operation. In former ages complex co-operation far more important than now because in these days we do so much by machinery.

The disadvantages of the division of labour are two.

I. Men are supposed to become of restricted capacity, by concentrating their attention upon one kind of operation only, – or a man becomes worth only the tenth part of a pin. Tho' a man's special technical skill may be very limited that does not seem to operate in an evil manner upon his general capacities, and the union of men in large factories, their living in large towns where their ideas are in constant agitation seems entirely to tend to the increase of intelligence, and in that way we may explain the superior intelligence of a factory hand to a country labourer.[10]

II. The second disadvantage of the division of labour is that the industrial system of society becomes highly complicated and delicately connected, so that any disturbance of supply and demand produces distress in one branch or other and it becomes difficult for any man thrown out of employment in one small branch to maintain himself in any other branch. That is an unquestionable evil and is an almost necessary result.

Next time to *Capital*.

Note A (1)

I have often thought of these curious facts in relation to labour and have tried to account for them; but I think the "historical accident" theory is, after all, sufficient to account for the origin of all those cases which are not easily traceable to the existence of some natural cause – such as collieries in the neighbourhood of coal. But when you have accounted for their origin by historical accident there remains to account for the remarkable fact that merchants, lawyers and trades people most should continue to congregate thickly in particular spots. I do not think that "ease of transporting parts of a watch" is a happy typical solution of the problem. A theory of mutual convenience will not apply, I think, except in such cases as the proximity of natural agents. It might conceivably apply in the case of the watchmakers too: but it would not apply to the grocers and sugar dealers and fishmongers. They don't operate together for mutual convenience, but for individual convenience, and in securing individual convenience they seek to meet the public convenience. Now, an expression which I heard the other day seems to me to clear up the whole matter. "If you want to succeed as a butcher open a shop next door to a

---

[10] Smith, *Wealth of Nations*, book v, chapter I, part III; II, 267–9.

butcher". "Historical accident" accounts for a certain butcher setting up in business in a particular locality. He acquires a reputation – which, another butcher envying him, causes another shop to be opened in close proximity. The neighbourhood then begins to have a reputation for good meat and also for larger choice. Then in the struggle for existence the butchers live as near to one another as possible and the result is that people get good meat. e.g. The Abattoir – Manchester; the Shambles, Sheffield, and indeed thus probably arise all the *special* markets.This I think accounts for the existence of markets such as Shude Hill,[11] etc., where there are long departments devoted to meat, etc. etc. – for all these markets now housed in the buildings had a local existence long before they were so covered in.

Historical accident in most cases accounts for the origin of this curious division of labour. But I think *close competition* accounts for the growth of the division itself.[12]

H.R.

LECTURE VII

CAPITAL

Nov. 19/75.

Capital forms the third requisite of production and is almost on a level with the other two – in fact, practically on a level with them except that, as Bentham remarked, labour must have preceded capital.[1] From land and labour everything proceeds, but in the actual state of things in the present day we always use some capital in production; so that it now takes its place as one of the three requisites. Until quite recently I was never able to ascertain the origin of the name capital. Of course it comes from the Latin Caput, but then in what way was that connected with the idea of head. I always thought of the *number** as the head, etc., but now it is made quite plain – in the early History of Institutions by Henry Maine[2] – that it is derived from the name of cattle [ancient way of

[11] Shude Hill, Manchester 4, runs from the top of High Street to Rochdale Road.

[12] This note was added by Rylett as his own comment on the lecture, apparently at a later date, since the two pages on which it is written are numbered separately from the continuous pagination of the manuscript.

[1] Jeremy Bentham (1748–1832), *Manual of Political Economy* (1793–5). See W. Stark, *Jeremy Bentham's Economic Writings*, 3 vols (1952–4) I, 226.

* *principle* ?   (H. R.)   [*sic*]

[2] Sir Henry J. S. Maine, *Lectures in the Early History of Institutions* (1875). See Vol. V, Letter 709, n. 1, p. 000.

trading] = hence chattel, local term for movable goods. French cheptel. English cattle. So we inherited the word capital. You can't imagine a better instance of capital than a stock of oxen, because they form the most valuable source of sustenance and food and are useful as draft animals.

Then, *Capital* may be regarded as temporary subsistence in the first place. It is remarked by James Mill that if a man makes his living by hunting wild animals he must keep a stock of food in hand sufficient to cover the average duration of a hunting excursion.[3] In the agricultural state more capital is required because in some parts of the world the harvest only comes once a year, whereas there are several harvests in some other parts of the world. But in a temperate region you must have nearly a year's stock of food in hand. If not labour will have to be given in providing food in some other way – perhaps by fishing. This is something of the case in Norway.[4]

How have P. Economists defined capital? A simple description is "an accumulated stock of the produce of labour applied to provide production or facilitate production."[5] It is doubtful how far – if a man merely lays up a stock to provide for his whole life and does nothing after – it is doubtful how far that can be called capital. Of course a number of definitions have been given. Fawcett says "Capital is every kind of wealth which in any way assists the production of wealth".[6] McCulloch's definition is "that it consists of those portions of the produce of industry which may be directly employed either to support human beings or to facilitate production."[7] The following is a statement of the use of capital: What capital does for production is to afford shelter, protection, tools, and materials which work requires: and to feed and otherwise maintain labourers during the process.

Perhaps we might get rid of a few absurd ideas connected with capital.

1st. Capital doesn't consist solely of money: little important connection between them. We are accustomed to speak of capital in the form of it. A man is said to have a capital of £50,000 engaged in a business or going to put into something. Then it might seem as if the capital were the 50,000 sovs., and it is no doubt quite true that capital does take the form of money for a short period, but it is only a passing form, as it were, only a mode of transfer. If the man ever sees his £50,000 it would probably only

[3] Mill, *Elements of Political Economy*, p. 9. This passage from James Mill is quoted in all editions of *T.P.E.*, although in the first edition Mill is not identified as its author. Cf. *T.P.E.*, first edition, p. 215; fourth edition, p. 224.

[4] Jevons's choice of Norway as an example probably sprang from his having spent the summers of 1872, 1873 and 1874 there. Cf. LJ, pp. 258, 278 and 311.

[5] This definition varies in form, though not in substance from those which Jevons gave in *T.P.E.*, p. 223 and the *Primer of Political Economy*, p. 46.

[6] In the fourth edition of Fawcett's *Manual* (1874) this passage reads 'every kind of wealth, which in any way assists future production, has been, in this chapter, described as capital . . .' (p. 41).

[7] Cf. McCulloch, *Principles of Political Economy*, fifth edition (1864) p. 47.

be in drawing them out or paying wages; so that it is plain that money is only one of a multitude of forms of capital. It measures and distributes, but does not constitute it. We shall see this most clearly if we consider that the money of a country is only a small amount of the property of the state [160 millions of money, but that only a small fraction of the property of the country.] I have no hesitation in saying that to obtain a correct notion of capital is the greatest difficulty in P.E. In fact, I have very little doubt that nobody has ever truly defined it and said precisely when property is capital and why it is capital and got clear of difficulties.

Perhaps one of the best ways of looking at the matter is to follow Mill in his fundamental propositions. [8]

I.   "Industry is limited by capital", and he goes on to remark that this is a proposition so evident as to be taken for granted in many common forms of speech, that to apply labour to anything is to apply capital, and to apply capital is to apply labour. Now I think this is open to serious objection. I don't say it is absolutely false; but it is quite false in the unguarded manner in which it is stated here because as Adam Smith remarks, the same quantity of capital may support very different numbers of labourers in different kinds of employment; or different modes of doing the same kind of work. [9] In fact the difference is so extreme that what will support one labourer only in one kind of work may support from one to two thousand or more labourers in another kind of work . . . has actually a range of something like 2,000 times or more.

Accordingly, suppose there is a fixed amount of capital, there is no limitation within that quantity of the number of labourers. To illustrate this we will take the various ways in which men are employed to convey goods. What is the simplest way of conveying goods? Carrying on the shoulders. But little food is required and a small frame is necessary for carrying it on his shoulders — five shillings this man's capital. Next, a horse and cart = carrier. What is his capital? Food of horse and himself and buildings and cart and horse. Equal to about £50. However, the last step is the railway system — in which the comparison between labourers and capital invested is almost lost. We must take the proportion between the amount invested and the men employed. I don't think you can put it at less than £2,000 per head, the amount of capital employed in each one's industry.

The result upon Mills' proportion is this: that the limitation of industry will entirely depend upon the proportionate amount of capital needed. However we shall come back to this upon a future occasion.

[8] Mill, *Principles*, book I, chapter v, pp. 63–4.
[9] 'Though all capitals are destined for the maintenance of productive labour only, yet the quantity of that labour, which equal capitals are capable of putting into motion, varies extremely according to the diversity of their employment' – Smith, *Wealth of Nations*, book II, chapter v; I, 340.

2nd Proposition: that capital is the result of saving. And Mill holds that somebody must save capital.[10] Either the person using it or somebody else must save it, and saving appears to be abstinence from consumption, the deferring of consumption. To save is to keep. Then, I apprehend, to keep is to preserve for a certain length of time. (Apple eaten, not-saved; not-saved, eaten.)

In the Third Proposition we have it stated that capital, tho' saved and the result of saving, is consumed, and Mill goes on to explain that consumption is essential to the idea of capital. Merely to keep a thing without using it up is to be a miser, not accumulating capital, but wasting the wealth of the country. Wealth laid up in that way is hardly capital, tho' it might at any moment be made capital. Mill goes on to say that saving does not imply that what is saved is not consumed, nor even necessarily that its consumption is deferred, but only that if consumed immediately it is not consumed by the person who saves it. You must see that here we are getting into difficulties, because I apprehend that you agree with me that to save it is to keep it a length of time; but here we are told that the consumption need not be deferred. So that between these two propositions there is direct contrariety — unless we are prepared to accept this qualification only, that the person who saved it need not consume it. Smith also thinks much the same.[11] Hence we come to this, that either capital must be kept a little time, or else be handed over to another person to consume; but that handing over is immaterial to the question. The whole of the phenomena of capital might go on in the case of a single family's industry where there was nobody else to hand it over to. One might take the case of people who settle in a new country. It is a common thing for a family to emigrate, to buy a farm of fresh land, settle down upon it, with a small capital which they eat up before they have got the ground at all into order, and then they have to struggle through the utmost distress and hard labour to raise their hut and get things into order. Consider such a family has already consumed its first capital. You will see that they consume immediately all that they can get — whatever food they can raise — and get thro' it as fast as they get it. But at the same time they are working away to raise their hut, clear the farm and improve it by degrees. Then there is no handing over of capital there, because they may be beyond the reach of neighbours. It is in such circumstances that the need of capital is most acutely felt, and it is almost always the case with new colonies that there is great distress at first.

Take another case nearly parallel: the slate quarries in Wales.[12] It is

[10] Mill, *Principles*, book I, chapter v, §§ 4–5, pp. 68–72.

[11] 'What is annually saved is as regularly consumed as what is annually spent, and nearly in the same time too; but it is consumed by a different set of people'. Smith, *Wealth of Nations*, book II, chapter III; I, 320.

[12] Cf. J. E. Cairnes, 'Co-Operation in the Slate Quarries of North Wales', *Essays in Political*

common for the quarryman to build his own house, i.e. he is allowed to take stone from the quarry, and he can cut it and work it himself, and does all the building himself after the hours of work. And in that way he eventually gets a house built with very little cost for window frames etc. Now when that house is finished it is worth, say £100. Where did the capital come from? I want to know this rather, whether there was any saving which resulted in his building his house? The more ordinary way in which a house is built is for the man to save money, and then when he has £100 he buys a house of that value.

As to the different kinds of capital that exist it is desirable to take Smith's statement. He speaks of the stock of the country – stock not synonymous with capital observe, but is divided into three parts.[13]

I.   Portion reserved for immediate consumption yielding no revenue. It consists of food, clothes, furniture, and generally all property a man has in ordinary use for his house. From that, you see, a man derives no profit in the way of monetary income. It is so much loss to him. The more money he spends on his furniture and clothes. This part Smith did not consider capital.

II.   The second part of the stock was called by Smith fixed capital. It was called fixed because it affords a revenue or profit without circulating or change of masters. It consists of four different groups. 1st. useful machines which facilitate labour; 2nd. profitable buildings, including all the buildings required in mills, breweries, shops or warehouses, docks etc. In fact it is difficult to discriminate between the buildings and machines. 3rd. improvements in land. By improvements in land I apprehend we mean any advantage which results from spending labour which is to repay itself in future. You would hardly call sowing land with corn an improvement of the land. Improvement of land is something that will last for years. As for example drainage and some kinds of manure: so *duration* makes improvement. 4thly the acquired abilities of workmen are mentioned by Smith. But it is so indispensable to distinguish between capital and labour and so difficult to do it, and it is so fearful a fallacy to talk of a man's labour being his capital that I rather pass this over for the present. There is nothing more false or misleading in Political Economy than to speak of a man's labour as his capital. Skill may be capital.

III.   Any portion of stock is called circulating capital which affords revenue by circulation, and that means the circulation that takes place in the case of money which is always passing from one person to another.

Then under circulating capital we can place first of all money, 2nd

---

Economy (1873) pp. 166–86.
[13] Smith, *Wealth of Nations,* book II, chapter I, 'Of the Division of stock'; I, 261–8.

stock of provisions in the hands of tradesmen, 3rd stock of raw materials, 4th work completed but not yet in use.

No doubt we are here in a great series of difficulties, because it would appear, according to Smith, that property in the use of a person is not capital. Then you will see in the *Theory* I have pointed out (p. 245)[14] that this distinction of Smith's between the first and other portions is exceedingly difficult to maintain. If the goods are in the consumer's hands they cease to be capital at once. If they are in the producer's hands they are capital, but it is easy to show that the distinction is quite immaterial and breaks down. Smith says "the whole stock of mere dwelling houses, (too,) subsisting at one time in the country makes a part of this first portion".[15] The stock laid out in the house, if it is the house of the proprietor, ceases to be capital: "a dwelling house as such contributes nothing to the revenue of its inhabitant", etc., Ch. I, B II. Then
income
McCullough [*sic*] in his derivation of the wealth of nations says the capital laid out in dwelling houses[16] is laid out as much . . . .*
Everybody will allow that *yon brewery*† is capital, because the proprietor makes a large sum of money in it. But in an earlier state of things every man had his own brewhouse and drank all his own ale. The case of a hotel, too, is a case of capital.

[Under the permissive Bill[17] each man would be his own brewer: this would probably be the case.]

---

[14] *T.P.E.,* first edition.

[15] Smith, *Wealth of Nations,* 1, 263.

[16] 'A dwelling-house is indirectly at least, if not directly, a source of revenue. To enable any useful or industrious undertaking to be carried on, those employed in it must be lodged: and it therefore follows, that the capital laid out in building houses for such persons is employed as much for the public advantage as if it were vested in the tools or instruments they make use of in their respective businesses' – Adam Smith, . . . *The Wealth of Nations,* edited by J. R. McCulloch (Edinburgh, 1863) p. 121, n. 2.

* ? (H. R.)

† [A picturesque pile to be seen from the college windows!] (H. R.)

[17] The Permissive Prohibitory Liquor Bill was first introduced in 1864 and promoted by the United Kingdom Alliance. It embodied the principle of local option, giving local authorities the power to control or prohibit liquor traffic in their own areas. Jevons's view of the matter was that 'in trying to pass a Permissive Bill the Alliance aimed at too much, and so hindered all reform' (LJ, p. 349). Cf. W. S. Jevons, 'On the United Kingdom Alliance and its Prospects of Success', a paper read before the Manchester Statistical Society on 8 March 1876, reprinted in *Methods,* pp. 236–52. For a full account of the development of licensing laws in the nineteenth century see G. B. Wilson, *Alcohol and the Nation* (1940) pp. 96–115.

LECTURE VIII
FIXED AND CIRCULATING CAPITAL
Nov. 26/75.

But the use of these words "fixed" and "circulating" by Smith is entirely different from the use of the words in subsequent writers. Smith mentions as the best instance of circulating capital, money, which he says produces no profit except it be parted with; and the stocks in the hands of shopkeepers are circulating capital simply because they are intended to be sold and got rid of, and the more quickly they are got rid of the more profitable for the shopkeepers, whereas the building of the shop, the machines employed in the factory, and many other things that are kept are fixed capital because they are not parted with, but on the contrary return a revenue by being kept.

It was Ricardo who introduced an entirely different meaning to these words "fixed" and "circulating", viz, that of the duration of the goods themselves;[1] to put it in the clearest light we may say there are three questions of duration:

1.   Duration in owners' possession.
2.   Duration of Existence [and then I shall
     afterwards point out a third sense, viz.]
3.   Duration in the same use.

All three are questions of time; but of these three

II.[2] the second sense is incomparably the most important. The duration refers to the length of time a thing will serve without being destroyed and this view of the matter has been practically accepted by all subsequent writers. Or at any rate they intended to accept it, if they do not always keep strictly to the doctrine. Accordingly you find in almost any work on the subject circulating capital is described as that which is destroyed by one use.* In Mill we find that plainly stated in his chapter on fixed and circulating capital. He says capital which in this manner fulfils the whole . . . .†[3] by a single use is called circulating capital, and it is called circulating because after being destroyed it has to be reproduced as it were: (not the same actual material of course, but

---

[1] 'According as capital is rapidly perishable, and requires to be frequently reproduced, or is of slow consumption, it is classed under the heads of circulating, or of fixed capital' – *The Works and Correspondence of David Ricardo*, vol. I, *On the Principles of Political Economy and Taxation*, edited by Piero Sraffa (Cambridge, 1951) p. 31.

[2] 'II' added here in the margin of the original manuscript.

* *one* use=most transient form, but not necessarily the *only* form.   (H. R.)

† ?   (H. R.)

[3] 'Capital which in this manner fulfils the whole of its office in the production in which it is engaged by a single use is called Circulating Capital' – Mill, *Principles*, book I, chapter VI, § I, p. 91.

another portion of material has to be made to take its place.) Thus when one harvest is eaten up we must produce another one; when coal is burnt in a furnace we must immediately have a new supply of coal to keep the engines going. A great quantity of what we call materials are in the same class, for instance take soap. You don't use soap more than once over. The portion you use goes away and you have to have a constant supply of soap. All these are cases of circulating capital. On the other hand fixed capital consists of durable things. It would not do to say that every durable thing was fixed capital, but we may say that all fixed capital is durable including all machines which last long, all buildings we may employ for a length of time. Such things as boats, again, and ships, a railway, tools, roads, docks. This is the almost unanimous doctrine of economists. For instance Chevalier calls a plough fixed capital; harvest circulating capital. [4] In Fawcett's manual you will find an enumeration of several instances of fixed capital. As he observes, the one portion of capital does not produce its effect in the same way as other portions, [5] but his doctrine is so every similar to that of Mill, that we need not enter upon it minutely.

Now the only objection which one can raise to this doctrine is this, that it leaves out so far an immense number of intermediate cases, that it professes to make one well defined class of circulating and one well defined class of fixed capital, whereas there are other kinds of capital which under that description would be neither one thing nor another. For instance, you can begin with things that last a day only and go on to things that last days, months, years. In short it is entirely a question of degree. Now would you suggest to me some kind of capital which lasts only a single day. Shellfish on some parts of the coast. Women gather cockles and bring them back, and then they are capital, but they won't keep long, and so have to be sold at once, and thus are very circulating capital. Then as to two or three days, some kinds of garden produce. Then for a few weeks, a file. For two or three years duration, oxen. And we may easily go on to cases for ten years. A case of infinite (practically so) duration, a house well built: public buildings. Railway works, canal works, may be considered very durable: a railway tunnel, too. One good instance of fixed capital is the new river cut, which was made by Sir Hugh Middleton in the reign of Queen Elizabeth, which has been conveying water ever since [6] – so that that was a most perfect instance of the investment of labour in a fixed form: of course it requires renewals, repairs

---

[4] Michel Chevalier, *Cours d'Economie Politique fait au Collège de France*, 3 vols (1842–50) tome iii, *La Monnaie*, pp. 364–5. See Vol. III, Letter 316, nn. 1 and 4, p. 208.

[5] Fawcett, op. cit., pp. 41–4.

[6] Sir Hugh Middleton (1560?–1631), goldsmith and merchant, responsible for the construction of the 38-mile New River Canal built during the reign of James I to increase London's water supply by bringing water from Chadwell and Amwell, Herts., to a reservoir at Islington.

and alterations – which somewhat modify the fixedness of the capital.

III.   Duration in the same use – that you won't find in books, because I am not sure how far it is of importance. It simply means this, that some articles are capable of conversion from one use to another use to a great extent; whereas other articles, when once formed into their particular shape are devoted to that use for ever afterwards, and if they fall or are not valuable in that use, they won't be valuable at all. It is the difference of what we may call negotiability in business matters which is very important to be taken into account in many business operations. If you invest money in a mine, it is divided into many operations – some sunk in the workings underground, another portion is invested in the pumps and engines for draining and various employments. Now if a mine fails to reach metal, as is usually the case, the consequence is that the money sunk in the ground is utterly lost, because there is no use for holes underground, whereas the pipes and implements sold off at a moderate reduction of
                  pumps
value can be applied to other purposes. Or compare a portable engine with the threshing machine which has been employed very hard at work. The portable engine can work the steam plough or a threshing machine. It may be used for an indefinite number of purposes, so that if it is not wanted for threshing it is sold for some other use. But you can't find any purpose to which a threshing machine could be put if there were no corn to thresh. The same occurs again in buildings. If you put up a building in town of a peculiar character for some particular purpose, and it fails to return profit in that way, then you will probably have to sell it at a great loss because it is not adapted to different purposes; but if you build a shop – if you want to go into the grocery business, and build a shop to carry on that, and then wish to get rid of it, the probability is that the shop will serve just as well for many other kinds of trade, so that you lose nothing. One peculiar case of that I mentioned a little while ago – viz. rising out of the communistic estates in the United States. They have built buildings in which the communists lived together. They found this great obstacle, that if they built once all these large buildings and had to move, they could not sell them. [7] So that is a case where capital was sunk for one use and cannot return for other use. However, that is less important than the other two, especially the second one.

Now I apprehend that the first sense of circulation, that of Smith, is of no consequence at all: that it breaks down altogether because it is a mere accident of things whether they remain in the same person's use or not. It

[7] Evidently a reference to the experimental communistic settlements established by the Owenite Movement in America during the 1820s: notably New Harmony, the community founded by Robert Owen in Indiana in 1825. For a detailed study, see J. F. C. Harrison, *Robert Owen and the Owenites in Britain and America* (1969).

is easy to point out things in recent times at any rate, railway shares for instance. I want to know whether the railway shares are fixed or circulating capital? Now a share means a share in the whole property of the railway. If a person owns £1,000 worth of stock in L.N.W. is that fixed or circulating? That means to say that you hold a 30,000th part of everything in the possession of the company – parts of which are circulating, but most of which is fixed capital. But a man holds a 30,000th part of this stock and the general stock is fixed. But it is by no means necessarily fixed in the sense of Smith, because men may buy and sell as often as they like. The changes in the proprietorship of a large company of that sort are or might be very considerable. Then there are other things that frequently change hands – such as machinery. Machinery is often bought for a particular purpose – as a stationary engine is bought to do a particular kind of work, and is often sold again to another particular kind of work. But there is one good instance of fixed capital which may change hands – railway waggons are quickly worn out; and again there is no reason that they should remain in the same ownership. It is common to hire them out. But there is one particular substance that seems to be the principal example *altogether of the complexity of moving capital** – there is one thing that is most fixed and most circulating, namely money. Money forms a puzzle – what Bacon would call a . . . .* [8] instance, because it is certainly most circulating in Smith's sense because people are so fond of spending what they have in their pockets, but tho' easily spent by the individual it is exceedingly fixed in duration – because we must look at the whole interval that elapses on the average between the taking of the gold and the eventual loss of it, either by accidentally dropping it into the sea, or by rubbing it away or dissolving it chemically. On Page 231 of the *Theory* I have pointed out that if one per cent of the gold in use is rubbed away in the course of a year, the duration of gold will be a 100 years; ½ per cent 200 years and so on. [9] There is no accurate means of deciding what is actually the wear. Some have given estimates of the average wear, but there is no reason for giving much confidence to them. I should say as good a guess as one could make would be ½ per cent of the whole stock of gold and silver employed – of plate and jewellery. If so the average investment of capital in that will be 200 years. In latter times, I dare say, the destruction is increased rather; silver is being used for electro plating and that might increase the loss.

* together of the fixity and of the moving of capital?   (H. R.)

* ?   (H. R.)

   [8] Jevons was here referring to one of the twenty-seven types of 'Prerogative Instance' listed and discussed by Bacon in the *Novum Organum* – probably 'Bordering Instances' since according to Bacon 'they are those which exhibit species of bodies that seem to be composed of two species, or to be rudiments between one species and another' – Bacon, *Works,* ed. Spedding and Ellis (1858) IV, 169.

   [9] *T.P.E.,* p. 241.

Then, I think we come to this conclusion, that the circulation from owner to owner is of no account at all in an economical point of view and we must look at the nation as owning the aggregate of its own property as it were. Whoever owns the shares of the L.N.W. railway, the nation certainly does hold them, and the nation has sunk labour in that railway and cannot get labour out of it except it repays its cost.

Then returning to the Second. We must go a little more into it. And the principal point is to form a clear notion of the investment of capital apart either from the capital or from its duration. In short there are three things. There is:

1.   Amount of Labour.
2.   Interval between exertion and enjoyment.
3.   Amount of investment.

Or, if you like, you can put it into the form of money. There is 1st the money, 2 the time invested, and 3 the amount of investment.

But we must remember that the third is the product of the other two and is a quantity of a quite different nature. In short amount of investment = money + time.[10] So that it is a quantity of different nature involving both money and time. You will see it very obviously in this way, that if you lend £100 for two years, you are deprived of the money to the same extent as if you lent £200 for one year. The same thing, exactly, arises in putting money into business. If you invest money in the making of goods to the amount of £200 for one year, you are deprived of the use of your capital to the same extent as if you put £100 in and didn't get it out for two years.

Accordingly when we sum up as it were the investment which takes place in any particular kind of work we must begin at the beginning and estimate whatever labour is spent upon the undertaking and the length of time which it has to be left in the occupation, as it were. Take, for instance, the case of sinking a coal mine. Suppose it is very deep, it may take three years to sink the shaft. We won't speak of the rent of the land, but look merely at the labour that is spent upon ultimately getting coal out of the coal mine. Suppose you mark off the years, we first of all have the cost of sinking the mine or shaft – that increases the deeper it gets – so that the investment of labour will go on something in this way:[11]

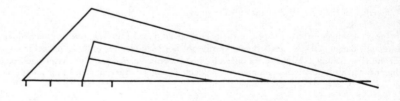

Then is this money spent in sinking the shaft fixed or circulating? Is the money got out again at all? It is if the mine is productive, and let us suppose that the mine lasts thirty years, then we may represent the repaying of this capital by the line nearly continuously falling, so the capital has to be repaid by profits extending over 30 years. Then there are various other expenses required in the coal mine. The engines for pumping purposes, etc. You can't call that circulating capital because every part lasts a long time; we might say, for instance, that the machinery would last half the time and that would have to be paid in half the time. There is another portion sunk in the timbering of the mine. That would be circulating because it gets crushed and often rots away very quickly. Then the horses used would be circulating; and coming down to the wages of the hewers of coal, – or take first the tools employed by them. That is comparatively circulating because the tools wear out quickly. Then we come to the hewers' wages and how much is that circulating? It is circulating to the extent of the turning over the price obtained for the coal, which is sometimes stocked and kept a year or more. As far as possible the coal is used and sent away to the places where it is burnt. Then I should think if we said six weeks that would be a fair average, that is to say, there is an average investment of six weeks of the wages of the hewers – then, that is decidedly circulating.

Thus in any particular industry the whole expenditure has to be in this way analysed in the various degrees of circulating or duration, and any company or firm whatever wanting to know its financial position ought really to take the minutest account of the different duration of their expenditure. It is a question of very great difficulty in an accountant's business, and it is here much fraud arises. It is a difference of what is called capital and current expenditure. Every company and works is spending money, but that money may be reproducing itself in a short or a long time; but it is a very nice question in auditing the accounts of a company, to decide whether that company is taking proper account of capital which has been expended previously. And the way in which it is practically worked out, as far as possible, is to allow for depreciation or wear and tear, or putting money to a reserve fund or sinking fund. There are various expressions, but they all mean this, that money which had been invested in a fixed form has been worn out by use gradually, so that after a time that capital will have to be replaced out of the profits of the business.

---

[10] From the context it is clear that this should read 'money x time'. Cf. *T.P.E.*, p. 232.
[11] Cf. the diagrams in *T.P.E.*, pp. 230 and 231.

Read Mills 4th Fundamental Proposition, and we will endeavour to get at the bottom of that — if we can.

Read all he says about capital, also Chapter VII of the Theory.[12]

LECTURE IX

ON MILL'S FOURTH PROPOSITION

Dec. 3/75.

We will discuss Mill's 4th proposition, not because I believe in it myself, but because other people do; and because it forms a kind of exercise in following out the nature of capital. This proposition is to the effect that what supports and employs productive labour is the capital expended in setting it to work and not the demand of purchasers for the produce of labour when completed. Or, as he more briefly and distinctly expresses it: "demand for commodities is not demand for labour".[1] The demand for commodities, he says, determines the direction of industry but not the more or less of the labour itself.

Here, I would observe, by the way, we have a clear instance of his meaning in the first proposition about capital as limited by industry. He says the more or less of labour does depend on the amount of capital devoted to the sustenance of labour.[2]

Now, as I said, some people believe this to be a true proposition and Mill thinks so much of it himself as to treat it as the keystone of the subject; but allows that very few economists have kept the truth in view. To common apprehension it is a paradox, and even of political economists of reputation I can hardly point to any except Ricardo and Say who have kept it in view.[3] Other people, he thinks, speak of purchasing commodities as if it was employing labour, whereas Mill says it does not employ labour.

Now that is one of the most extraordinary paradoxes ever put forth and to accept it involves a total misapprehension of the whole subject of capital, because capital is a mere question of advancing the sustenance of the worker whilst his work is going on; so that unless there was a demand for the commodity to be produced the capital would have no use whatever.

[12] i.e. the chapter on 'Theory of Capital'.

[1] Mill, *Principles*, book I, chapter v, § 9, p. 78.

[2] 'The demand for commodities determines in what particular branch of production the labour and capital shall be employed; it determines the *direction* of the labour; but not the more or less of the labour itself, or of the maintenance or payment of the labour. These depend on the amount of the capital, or other funds directly devoted to the sustenance and remuneration of labour' – Mill, loc. cit.

[3] This sentence is almost a direct quotation from Mill, loc. cit., p. 80.

I hardly know which way to attack it first of all, but let us consider what takes place when you purchase any goods. Take as an instance the purchase of a certain number of chairs and tables which you want. Now, there are two ways in which you might get them. You may go to a shop where they are found ready made for the purpose, or you can employ a workman yourself in your own house. Of course that is an inconvenient way. But the question is what is really the difference between these two means of doing it?

The point is this: that when you have to make the chairs yourself you have to wait while they are being made, so that you are advancing the sustenance of the work-people during that time. You become a capitalist to that extent, and are capitalising your income so far. On the other hand if you buy them ready made the upholsterer has advanced the sustenance of the workman for a certain number of months before. He cannot tell exactly how long goods are on hand; but you might say from 6 to 9 months between the time he begins goods and sells them, or it might be less, very much less than that in particular cases.

Now Mill states that in the ordinary capitalist mode of producing things two funds are required. There is the fund of the purchaser and there is also the fund of the capitalist. [4] Accordingly he thinks that there is a sort of absorption of double funds which in another mode of applying the money would be saved, and he comes to this conclusion: "A person applying his income to the direct support of labour increases the sustenance of the working class." [5] He contrasts the results of two cases, a consumer employing labourers in his own gardens or grounds; and secondly the same consumer diverting his income to the purchase of velvet. And the question is whether the difference of these two modes of expending his income affects the interests of the labouring classes. Mill holds that the former mode is most beneficial, because then he says there are two funds employed in the maintenance and remuneration of labour. Suppose an annual income of £500 spent in either of these two modes: (1) gardening, (2) velvet makers. Then Mill says if the £500 goes to the gardeners they get that sustenance. [6] Of course velvet makers do not get

[4] Mill, *Principles*, book I, chapter v, § 9, pp. 82–3.

[5] Mill, loc. cit., p. 83: '. . . a person does good to labourers, not by what he consumes on himself, but solely by what he does not so consume. If instead of laying out 100l. in wine or silk, I expend it in wages, the demand for commodities is precisely equal in both cases . . . but the labourers of the community have in the latter case the value of 100l. more of the produce of the community distributed among them.'

[6] The argument here and in the ensuing pages closely foreshadows that developed by Jevons in his *Principles of Economics,* chap. xxiv, 'Mill on Capital', pp. 126–33.

As Professor H. G. Johnson has pointed out 'what Mill seems to have had in mind is a rather crude conception of the process of production in terms of stages, crude insofar as all commodities are assumed to take only one stage for production and services to take two stages (i.e., labour into commodities, and commodities into labour services). In static analysis this amounts to the that sustenance in that case. But the velvet makers' capital must be at least £500, and that capital must be employed in supporting somebody else, so that there is £500 of that goes to other trades. In this way it is there are two funds.

The answer I should give is this. There is a confusion of two different kinds of funds. One is an annual income, i.e. the purchaser's income; the other is a standing capital which is alternately put into goods and then taken out when the goods are sold. The velvet maker no doubt makes velvet to the extent of £500 and he spends that sum upon it. But then he only spends it for a temporary purpose, and at the end of a few months he receives the same sum back from the purchasers of velvet. Therefore all the velvet maker does is to anticipate the velvet buyer and have it made before it is actually known he will buy it.

Now the same thing exactly would happen in the case of a garden. If you wanted one ready made you would have some capitalist to make the garden itself. That actually takes place. There is no difference whatever between the two cases. The builder invests his money in the wages of gardeners to make the garden ready for the inhabitant, just as the velvet maker does in making the velvet before it is wanted. Thus Mill's error arises from the fact that the purchaser spends his income to await the result himself. If I build my own house I may go and dwell in it myself, and may wait while I have gardeners to make the gardens in proper order, and during that time I am spending money without result. I am investing capital therefore.

And the whole difference between these two may be done away with if you really look to the question of time, and suppose the man to save his money up and invest it through the banks in some other kind of business.

Say it takes six months for the goods to be made. There is the velvet.

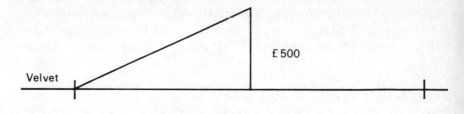

assumption that the labour co-efficient of production of services is double that of commodities' ('Demand for Commodities is *not* Demand for Labour', *Economic Journal*, 59 (1949) 535). Jevons's critique of Mill essentially depends on the implicit assumption that no such difference exists between the production process for commodities and that for services.

The man has an income constantly accruing of £500 in the half year. Then it accrues gradually in [   ]⁷ during the six months. Now, we have two possible cases, viz. where the capitalist makes it and gradually invests the £500 in the making of velvet during the six months. Then suppose the purchaser to be awaiting the completion of this velvet, he will have his income in the bank, the result of which is that his capital will accrue and be in the bank to the extent of £500 during the same period. I am now supposing that he is awaiting the velvet, which he wanted from the first, until it is ready. Then the capitalist maker of these things is investing £500 at the same time the purchaser is accumulating the same amount. Then I mean to say the real working of the capital of the country is not affected at all, because money in banks goes into trade in some way or other. Or you may put it in this way: A man goes and buys velvet to the amount of £500: he must have accumulated that money, and if he was not employing velvet makers himself, he would be leaving it in his bank, awaiting the time when he wanted to purchase.

There is a further difficulty which Mill gets into where he says that in one case there must be double employment because if you employ gardeners you employ people who supply them with food. If, Mill says, £500 goes to gardeners, the gardeners spend their money in food; so the food producers are also supported.

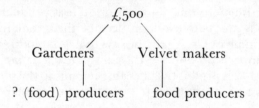

He seems to have forgotten altogether that the velvet makers wanted food; for certainly if the money went to them they would employ food producers.

The result simply is this: that one of the funds is a standing capital sum. This is put in and out of trade and turned over in a certain length of time and all I would admit is that this standing capital if not regained in one trade may be useful in improving the mode of industry in other trades. I am far from denying that capital is very valuable to industry, but it is so not because it employs labour exactly, so much as that it enables them to practise their work in a more advantageous manner by the use of machinery and various kinds of preparations. Indeed I believe if it were fully gone into the whole idea of capital [would be found to be]*

⁷ This word is indecipherable.
* ? Notes imperfect. These words are inserted fr. memory. (H. R.)

furnishing employment for labour. It is the workmen who employ themselves on their own work and the capital does nothing but enable them to do that between the beginning and the accomplishment of the work.

One or two questions we must allude to before passing on.

1. Whether goods in the possession of a consumer are capital or not. According to all the usual definitions they would not be. They fall under the stock devoted to immediate consumption by Smith and all other economists who define capital as wealth devoted to facilitate production.[8] But what you have in your own dining room is not used to facilitate production according to them. That is a very convenient arbitrary definition, but I don't believe it stands the test of close examination, because what is it after all that one does produce? I object to the very fundamental idea that there is such a thing as unproductive labour in the sense taken by certain P. Economists. It is said by Mill that labour is productive and unproductive, and they have laboured to make a distinction between these. Unproductive labour is that which leaves no tangible result apparently, which may give satisfaction at the moment like a song or musical performance or work of a housemaid, but which leaves nothing behind as it were; or, taking the more technical language of Mill, does not add to the accumulation of material wealth. Productive labour on the other hand is that which adds to the material wealth of the country. Accordingly to make a chair or table is productive labour. To make a garden is productive labour, because there remains permanently some sign or evidence of it. Again, he says that what indirectly adds to the wealth of a country is productive; thus, if you teach a man how to make a chair or table, that is productive, because it tends to the ultimate increase of the collection of furniture in the country, but to take an illustration often used,[9] . . . .*

Thus there is no essential difference between these. I should say there is no such real difference whatever, because the ultimate production to which we look is the production of utility. The production of employ-

---

[8] Smith, *Wealth of Nations*, book II, chapter I; I, 261.

[9] Mill, *Principles*, book I, chapter III, § 3, pp. 48–50: 'Thus, labour expended in the acquisition of manufacturing skill, I class as productive, not in virtue of the skill itself, but of the manufactured products created by the skill, and to the creation of which the labour of learning the trade is essentially conducive. The labour of officers of government in affording the protection which, afforded in some manner or other, is indispensable to the prosperity of industry, must be classed as productive even of material wealth because, without it, material wealth in anything like its present abundance, could not exist. Such labour may be said to be productive indirectly or mediately, in opposition to the labour of the ploughman and the cotton-spinner, which are productive immediately. They are all alike in this, that they leave the community richer in material products than they found it; they increase, or tend to increase, material wealth.'

The illustrations used by Jevons are not taken from Mill.

* Something missing here from the notes. (H. R.)

ment, or the warding off of pain is the ultimate result of all our labour, and it is of no consequence in what form that comes about. You may take this instance: those who contribute to a performance on the pianoforte consist partly of the men who made it; and next to the performer who performs. Now, Mill would call productive labour that of the maker of the piano; but that of the performer unproductive. Now can there be anything more groundless than this distinction, because what is the purpose of the piano, but to be used in the production of enjoyment?

If this is so, this distinction between productive and unproductive labour becomes imaginary. If it were not so the physician's would be unproductive, although the pastrycook's would be productive labour.

Now music is a necessary of life; and I don't allow, therefore, that the producer of music is an unproductive labourer.

It would seem, therefore, that this class of P. Economist seems to look upon labourers as so many machines producing goods, as if it were for the sake of production of them, whereas, we must look to the consumption of the goods and the warding off of evil as the real result of all labour. In that way I don't really believe in the distinction between productive and unproductive consumption. I should say, and it seems obvious, that all consumption is unproductive. Consumption in itself is simply the destroying of utility (not absolutely perhaps, but speaking of the consumption of food by the person who eats it.)

Now there is no necessary connection between consumption and production whatever. People must live, whether they work or not, so that consumption is the end of all industry; and as regards capital – to repeat once more – it is not the capitalist who finds the food for the working people ultimately. He only advances that consumption which is absolutely requisite for them to carry on and await the result.

Then to return again to this point: are goods awaiting consumption capital or not? We can hardly say they are capital in the ordinary sense of the word, but they have capital invested in them, and it is really immaterial in many cases whether they be in the consumer's possession or not. I could take many cases to prove that there is really no distinction. One is as follows: In primitive agricultural countries such as Norway or Sweden, the farmers actually eat up the corn which they produce on their own fields, put it in their own barns, thresh it out and grind it themselves and make their own bread, so that they hold the whole stock of corn upon which they live. If so according to the P. Economists, it wouldn't be capital, because it is in their possession. In England, as everybody knows, it is not usual to keep your own stock of corn in your own house. In general, poor people don't and can't keep stock in hand. The result is that the stock is held by corn merchants and millers, and it is a regular trade to hold corn, and to a great extent it is the trade of the farmers. They keep it and sell it gradually thro' the year. Now to them the corn is capital. They must receive interest on it in the increased price they get by holding it. If, then, every farmer and miller so far as he holds it calls it capital why should not the little holder be a capitalist to that extent – for he would save the profit that would accrue to somebody else.

Then you come to this, that the house you build is capital if you don't live in it, and not if you do. Suppose two houses of £100 a year rent and suppose the owners to live each in his own house, they are not capital. But suppose them to change houses, then each will owe the other a rent of £100 a year for the house. But all they would have to do would be to exchange receipts. The same thing extends itself to furniture and all things else we possess. Certainly all this would make us suppose that all wealth was capital. But certainly some wealth can exist without giving it the advantage of capital. That is to say suppose you have a stock of goods that is not wanted and has to wait for consumption more than the receiving time, then I mean to say that does not serve the purpose of capital. It is made at one time and consumed at another.*

LECTURE X

POPULATION

Dec. 10/75.

Population is really a very different branch, but it is quite essential to understand the general problem which we ultimately come to of the progress of nations – the cause of poverty or prosperity. This subject was brought before the public for the first time in a distinct form by Malthus in his essay upon population published in 1798,[1] since which time there have been many other editions. It is not to be supposed that Malthus entirely discovered the very germs of his own theory. As usually happens there were anticipations more or less distinct, and we find in the writings of Hume even,[2] and of Adam Smith,[3] Dr. Price,[4] Wallace,[5] and in the

---

* *Note.* These last sentences marked down the side were not lecture proper, but remarks at the conclusion of the lecture. (H. R.)

[1] Thomas Robert Malthus (1766–1834), *An Essay on the Principle of Population, as it affects the future improvement of Society, with remarks on the speculations of Mr. Godwin, M. Condorcet and other writers* (1798). All page references here are to the Royal Economic Society reprint, 1926.

[2] David Hume (1711–76), *Of the Populousness of Ancient Nations* (1752). See E. Rotwein, *David Hume. Writings on Economics* (Madison, Wisconsin, 1955) pp. 108–83.

[3] Smith, *Wealth of Nations*, book I, chapter VIII; 1, 66–88.

[4] Richard Price (1723–91), *An Essay on the Population of England from the Revolution to the Present Time* (1780).

[5] Robert Wallace (1697–1771), *A Dissertation on the Numbers of Mankind, in Ancient and Modern Times* (1753).

writings of Jeremy Bentham[6] a distinct assertion of the general principle, namely, that to increase the numbers of a nation you must begin by increasing their prosperity. The whole point in dispute in fact is which is cause and which effect. Is a nation numerous because it is prosperous, or is it prosperous because it is numerous. Previous to the time of Malthus almost everybody thought that you must make a nation strong and prosperous by making it numerous, and the policy of governments and laws was distinctly directed to this end. It was thought well to put a tax on bachelors in the Roman law. And in various times in the middle ages down even to the present day some consideration is shown to those who make large additions to the population. Certainly it was not long ago put on the ground that they added to the number and the strength of the nation. Now Malthus took the precisely opposite view that to make a nation numerous you must make it prosperous, and then there is no doubt it will become numerous. And he took this view to almost an extreme extent, asserting that the tendency to numerical increase was so great that the larger part of the population would be upon the verge of famine.

But coming to his more particular statement he laid down two fundamental propositions:

1. That population tends to increase in a geometrical ratio.
2. Subsistence tends to increase in an arithmetical series.[7]

Assuming for a few minutes that these are true it is very easy to see that population must always tend to overcome subsistence.

An arithmetical series is one that always increases uniformly, $1000-1001-1002-1003$. A geometrical series goes by uniform multiplication, so if we start by one and multiply by 2 we get 1, 2, 4, 8, 16, 32, 64.

The difference between these two is shown in all kinds of results. Incidentally I might mention that all statistical and social matters ought properly to be regarded from the geometrical point of view.[8] The arithmetical point of view only occurs in the case of balance sheets; but all statistics, all facts relating to population have no meaning at all unless taken relatively, i.e. as regards the ratio one to another. However, it will be observed that if we proceed many steps in this geometrical series we soon get to very large numbers – in ten steps to 1024; and if we take ten steps in that other series ($1001-2-3$, etc.) I only get to 1010. Then having once overtaken the food supply we advance beyond it in a most alarming manner 1024, 2048, 4096, 32768, and here we have 32 times the population that can be subsisted.

---

[6] Bentham, *Manual of Political Economy; Supply without Burthen* . . . (1795). See Stark, *Jeremy Bentham's Economic Writings*, I, 272–3, 361–6.

[7] Malthus, *Essay on Population*, p. 14.

[8] Jevons adopted the geometrical mean for his calculation of index numbers in *A Serious Fall*; for his arguments in favour of this method, see *Investigations*, pp. 23–4.

Compound interest is another example of geometrical increase. And there is no doubt that when you follow out any case of geometrical increase it proceeds in a totally unlimited manner.

Then comparing these two propositions Malthus produces a constant tendency in all animated life to increase beyond the nourishment prepared for it.

But, as I said, this is hypothetical for the present. Of course we must ascertain the two positions before we adopt the conclusion drawn from that.

First, does population tend to increase in a geometrical ratio? Now, nobody asserts that in any part of the world are there any absolutely exact examples of this geometrical tendency, because so many causes interfere restraining the increase or disguising it. But I have no hesitation in saying that it is accurately true in a hypothetical point of view. There are two ways of proving it – a priori and posteriori.

The *a priori* way consists in saying that from other reasons it is to be expected that it would increase in that way. Now, I don't see the slightest difficulty in showing that a priori it must be so – because if you imagine a certain population to be planted in a certain area of country:

$$\boxed{200}$$

and 200 people settled there – then grant that in a certain number of years that will double in number, say 35 years, then in 35 years that 200 will have doubled and will occupy twice the area:

Now, what will happen in the next 35 years. Supposing there is no alteration in their physical condition – that they have an equal amount of land to spread over, no mountains or sterile land, or anything different from before? They must have equal area so that each 200 can spread over the same area that was spread over in the previous 35 years. What is there to prove apriori that this 200 will increase to 800, now? There must be something to make them act differently if they don't double as their fathers did:—

200	200
200	200

and then next to

200	200	200	200
200	200	200	200

Hypothetically, then, it cannot be denied this first proposition is true.

The *aposteriori* proof of it consists in furnishing statistics. Taking experience on a large scale and showing that where the hypothetical conditions remain somewhat the same, there is multiplication in this manner, and that where it does not occur it can be accounted for by the operation of other causes. Malthus used the aposteriori principle to a great extent and the greater part of the three volumes consists of a collection of statistics and facts tending to establish it.[9]

The *Second Proposition* is that subsistence tends to increase in an arithmetical series. There may be some approximation to truth in that, but it is a mistake to suppose that it can be altogether true or that Malthus can really have meant it to be accurate. I take it to be merely a rough way of saying that food cannot be increased much without a great increase of difficulty; or, in other words, that the increase of food is not proportional to the increase of labour.

That however is a point that we shall have to go into fully on the subject of rent and the *nature** of natural agents.

But we can easily see that there is some rude approximation to truth in the matter by considering that all physical agents, all natural materials are limited in quantity ultimately; that you cannot mention a substance of which the quantity is not finite; and that as regards food it really depends to a great extent upon the area open to cultivation, not merely upon the soil; but sunshine is absolutely requisite to vegetation. The sun's rays decompose carbonic acid and allow carbon to be...............[10] vegetation, so the ultimate limit of the supply of food must depend upon having an area where you have some sunlight at your command. There is no doubt that by various inventions and attempts at improvement we can very greatly increase the quantity of food proceeding from any particular area. That coming from the fields now is probably three or four times as much as it was in former ages. Then by manures we can effect a greater increase; so that it would almost seem as if

[9] The fifth edition, 'with important additions', of Malthus's *Essay on Population*, published in 1817, was the first to extend to three volumes. The 'important additions' did in fact consist largely of facts, statistical and otherwise, designed to prove the truth of Malthus's assertions about the power of population to increase.

* ? (H. R.)

[10] Gap in text of manuscript. The words left out were presumably 'utilised by'.

there is no definite limit to the amount of food produce in any one form. They say from the sewage farms they can raise several crops a year. But it is certain that that must be done by a great increase of labour for, otherwise, why is it that it is not usually done. Why is it we import corn? That we will go back to again when we come to natural agents.

Now, we look to the other side of the question – what it is which prevents population from increasing in the manner shown by the geometrical series. Malthus laid down two different classes of "checks" to population. [11]

The first were called *Preventive checks*. They consist in such as prevent population from coming into existence. They practically resolve themselves into prudence or the deferment of marriage to a later period of life. When we compare the main part of our English population with that of some of the continental nations we see the difference in that respect. A young carpenter who has just got through his apprenticeship and become a journeyman carpenter, and gets 30/-d per week, if he is only 21, 20, 19 or 18 marries straight off and before he is 30 has a large family of children. Well, there we see a total want of prudence, because he has a family to keep before he has laid up any stock of savings as a reserve fund. If he is fortunate and keeps his health and strength and gets good wages, everything goes well perhaps, but in a considerable proportion of cases, something will happen to the father. He may die long before many of his children are able to take care of themselves. But there can be no doubt that children are brought into the world by those who are unable to support them.

Whereas in France and Switzerland and a good many of the other continental countries there is the habit of deferring marriage until a man can show he has the means of sustaining a family or can take a farm. The result is a much slower rate of increase in the population.

Secondly we come to what are called the positive checks which might perhaps better be called the destructive checks, because they include all the causes which destroy population once brought into existence – including famines, diseases, extreme poverty, bad nursing of children, intentional infanticide, intemperance, occupations, severe labour, and finally wars. Now it is obvious that in different states of society these checks operate in various degrees but all to a great extent. One of the most common sources of loss of population is bad nursing. One wonders how in a primitive state of society we survived at all – possibly by the natural instinct of mothers.

Then in some countries there are institutions that undertake the care of

---

[11] Malthus, *Essay on Population*, pp. 62–3. Cf. Kenneth Smith, *The Malthusian Controversy* (1951); D. E. C. Eversley, *Social Theories of Fertility and the Malthusian Debate* (Oxford, 1959).

young children. A very large number of the juvenile population of France are taken to these institutions and only a mere fraction of them survive.

In England we know a great deal has been said of the increase of infant mortality: mothers going to work in the day, e.g., said to be an important cause.[12] In other portions of the world famines come in as one means of a check; and in fact in certain stages of society it is a normal check of population – a famine comes to be looked upon as a kind of natural event. In England we have so far got past that, that it seems an altogether unnatural occurrence for anyone to die of want of food. But we are shocked to hear of famines in India or Asia and forget that that is what has been happening since the beginning of things. It is not our doing. But it is civilisation that has made them remarkable. Of course war is, again, a normal state of things, in early societies. The North American Indians, for example, their only serious occupation, their only amusement, was war.

One of the most troublesome parts of the question is as to diseases – can they be said to keep down population? It is said it is like stopping one gap to all people to die out by another gap – if you save them from smallpox, they will take fever: the better way is to let diseases take them off as quickly as they like, for they are sure to take them sooner or later.[13] No doubt, the duration of life is greater now than during the previous century. There are no statistics available, but when we consider the plagues they used to have, black death, and all sorts of dreadful epidemics and compare them with the mild epidemics now it appears a fair presumption that the average duration of life would be shorter than it is now.

Then there is the way people live:—the way the Irish live, especially, in some of our large towns and in some parts of their own country, makes it a priori probable that they die fast.[14]

The general result which Malthus drew from his propositions etc. was, that there was no hope of the main body of the people being permanently elevated into a state of high civilisation, because so soon as they acquired increased means of subsistence, they would be sure to marry and multiply. That would bring down the rate of wages, increase the demand for food, and the cost of food, and would prevent them from being any better than they were in former days. The same notion was adopted by Ricardo who looked upon the natural rate of wages as the least which will

[12] Cf. Vol. V, Letters 708–10 and notes, pp. 161–7.

[13] Vaccination against smallpox was made compulsory in England in 1853, but controversy over its effectiveness continued for many years. See Tranter, op. cit., pp. 79–93, for an examination of the significance of medical advance as a factor in population growth.

[14] Jevons had put forward this hypothesis in his Presidential Address to Section F. of the British Association at its Liverpool meeting in 1870, and produced some statistical evidence to support it in an Appendix to that address; see *Methods*, pp. 208 and 213–16.

enable labourers to maintain themselves and keep up their numbers – and he meant mere necessaries of life, mere bread and cheese.[15] There is very little doubt that Malthus took too gloomy a view of things. He was interpreted as flying at the very constitution of society, and the kind of result to which he pointed was as follows:—every enlargement of our resources only tends to land us in a larger, it is true, but a more straightened [*sic*] population.

Next go on to the doctrine of distribution.

LECTURE XI

THE DOCTRINE OF DISTRIBUTION

The way in which different classes of the community receive different portions of the produce, or it may not be different classes always, but the same person may receive different portions in respect of different contributions to industry in a different capacity, as it were.

The three requisites of production were natural agents, labour and capital: the three corresponding portions of the produce are rent, wages and interest, and we have to consider each of these separately.

We may put it in this obvious way, that the total produce = rent + wages + interest. Now rent and interest are determined, at any rate according to the idea of some economists, separately; and wages form the principal portion which we have now to consider more particularly. This, in fact, introduces us to the principal problem of P.E. – how the share of the labourer may be increased to the utmost possible extent, or upon what principle the amount is regulated.

Now the word wages is a very ambiguous one, and bears at least three different meanings in different writings. It is commonly used to mean the money wages in which it is usually paid over to the labourers; but inasmuch as nobody eats gold or silver, or uses it for any purpose except paying it away again, it is obvious that the amount of the money is not the important thing if we can get at the absolute or real wages, consisting of the necessaries and luxuries, i.e. the total amount of commodities which labour can get. This is a complicated notion because different labourers don't buy the same commodities. The one man with a large family may

[15] Ricardo defined the natural price of labour as 'that price which is necessary to enable the labourers, one with another, to subsist and to perpetuate their race, without either increase or diminution' (*Principles of Political Economy and Taxation*, edited by P. Sraffa, p. 93.). Jevons's assertion that 'he meant mere necessaries' is not borne out by a reading of Ricardo who specifically referred to 'the quantity of food, necessaries and conveniences become essential to [the labourer] from habit'.

have to buy little else than bread; another man – a single man – may spend a large amount of his wages in amusements. It is therefore difficult to form a notion. Again the word has been used to mean the proportion of wages or the fraction of the total produce which the labourer obtains in *the bargain.** This, however, is the sense in which it has only occasionally been used by Ricardo.[1]

Most writers have really discussed the money wages and people practically do this – probably because it is very much more easy to discuss. We have records of the amount of money wages and we can easily find out whether they rise and fall, but to ascertain whether the real wages rise or fall is a difficult matter because you must take into account both the money wages, the respective amount of commodities purchased and the change of price of all those commodities. But it is quite clear that real wages may vary very considerably while the money wages would not vary. Indeed real wages vary according to the price of corn, and other goods affect them in the same way.

I believe there may be said to be two distinct theories now current as to the way in which wages are regulated – two rival theories. And the first has by far the most popular countenance at present, it having been adopted by Ricardo and Mill. It is called the wages fund theory. It is easy to explain chiefly because it is a truism. It arises from viewing wages as simply the price paid by the capitalist for the labour which he buys. It is a view of the subject arising from the capitalist point of view. We regard the labourer as not working for his own sake, as it were, as not the actual producer, but as being bought up and made into a mere servant of the capitalist. Hence the labourer's share depends entirely upon the competition of capitalists to obtain his services; so that we come to regard labour as a matter of supply and demand, and wages are governed by the laws of supply and demand – But in a very simple way, because assume on the one side a certain number of capitalists with a certain amount of capital, then they will not want to let that capital lie idle. They must invest it to avoid loss, and in investing it the very result is to pay it as wages directly or indirectly. The circulating capital of the country is always tending to take the form of wages and thus forms the demand for labour. Then the supply of labour is simply the whole labouring population who are competing for employment. Thus we get to a very simple formula,

$$\text{viz. that the average rate of wages} = \frac{\text{wage fund}}{\text{number of labs.}} = \frac{\text{circulating captl.}}{\text{labg. population}}$$

But there you see is a point to be considered. Does every labourer share equally in this? That resembles the question does every shareholder in a

* ? (H. R.)
[1] Cf. Ricardo, *Principles of Political Economy and Taxation*, edited by P. Sraffa, pp. 49–50.

company share equally? No. Each share does. But is each share on an equal footing or not? That is the first difficulty. Ricardo was aware of the difficulty, but he avoided it in a very clever and satisfactory way, namely, he disregarded it. He assumed that at any rate the greater number of labourers are upon a par: that they are common labourers, and that they have hardly more than enough just barely to sustain life.[2] Then such other labourers as there are with higher rates of wages are treated by him and also by Mill as sections, not to be worth consideration in this Theory.[3] The fact is that many parts of Ricardo's theory are sweeping hypotheses, etc. Now we know, as a matter of fact, that in England at the present time the wages of an able man vary from 10/- up to 50/-. Now when some receive five times as much as others it is rather arbitrary to put them on the same footing.

But – another difficulty: viz., does this circulating capital here mean the whole of the circulating capital of the country or does it not? It does not. Mill allows that in his first proposition about capital. "You find", he says, "that although capital limits industry it does not follow that industry always reaches the limit."[4] He distinctly asserts that capital may be laid by, and as a matter of fact we have abundant proof of that because we know there is such a thing as depression of trade when the banks are overflowing with money but they can't get anybody to spend it. The supply of corn may be large, but yet in a certain state of trade it is not applied to payment of wages, owing to want of confidence in the future of trade. We may accept that as a fact for the present. If so this wage fund does not mean the whole of the circulating capital, but it means – portion of circulating capital applied to the payment of wages.

Now this wage fund pretends to determine the rate of wages by dividing the wage fund by the number of labourers – but then you must know the *quantity* of the wage fund and the number of labourers. Let us assume that we know the number of labourers – then what is it that determines the rate of wages?*

Therefore I said this is a truism. It merely asserts that the rate of wages

[2] It would appear that Jevons was here permitting himself a looseness of expression which conveys the broad sense of what Mill and Ricardo wrote, but hardly gives them credit for the qualifications which they both expressed. Although Ricardo did not treat the causes of wage differences in his chapter 'On Wages' the well-known Section II of his chapter 'On Value' does contain the explicit statement – 'I must not be supposed to be inattentive to the different qualities of labour, and the difficulty of comparing an hour's or a day's labour, in one employment, with the same duration of labour in another.' – *Principles*, edited by P. Sraffa, pp. 20–1. After considering 'the laws which govern the remuneration of ordinary or average labour', J. S. Mill devoted a separate chapter to 'The Differences of Wages in Different Employments' – *Principles of Political Economy*, book II, chapter XIV – which Jevons later instructed his students to read. Cf. below, p. 64.

[3] Mill, *Principles*, book I, chapter V, § 2, pp. 65–6.

[4] Ibid.

* ?something missed here, I think.   (H. R.)

is the aggregate paid in wages divided by the number of labourers. But that is merely the way of taking an average.

The point of great importance is this, whether the high prices of commodities make high wages: and we might consider two different points of view.

1st   Whether high prices of food make high rates of money wages or not. This is a point of great practical importance, because you will always find trade unionists arguing that they must have high wages because necessaries are high. The question is whether, theoretically, it is possible to raise wages always when prices of food are raised. As a matter of fact we find that it is not so – that the rise in the price of corn has no effect in raising wages of labourers generally. That can be easily proved statistically. In fact if anything the effect is in a different direction. If corn rises in price there is a slight tendency in wages to fall. If the price of corn rises it reduces real wages earned by a certain number of hours work. The result therefore is that many labourers attempt to work longer hours or those who are working by piece work more vigorously. In short the supply of labour measured by the length of time and exertion increases when the price of corn is high, and then as there is a greater supply of labour the money rate tends to fall. Then the high price of corn reduces the free capital in the labour market: there is a tendency to throw labourers out of employment.

See Porter's quotation p.175 of Theory.[5]

Then again there rises this question – whether the wages of labourers in different parts of the country ought to be proportioned to the expense of living in these districts. It is more expensive in London than in a provincial town; more expensive in a provincial town than in a purely rural place. Has the labourer in London the right to demand higher wages than what are paid in other places?

Now, it is a question of what the labourer can get and what the employer is obliged to pay him.

Then in London, where prices are high, for living, the capitalist may or may not be obliged to pay higher wages, but the simple result is this, that if he wants his business to go on, he must pay high wages, and if he does not the business will collapse. The question practically occurred in

---

[5] 'Statements are given by Mr. Porter, in his "Progress of the Nation" (edition of 1847, pp. 454, 455) which show that when a sudden rise took place in the prices of provisions in the early part of this century, workmen increased their hours of labour or, as it is said, worked double time if they could obtain adequate employment' – *T.P.E.*, first edition, p. 175. The reference is to George Richardson Porter (1792–1852), *The progress of the nation in its various social and economical relations, from the beginning of the nineteenth century* (new edition, 1847).

connection with the shipbuilding trade. Capitalists constructed ship-building yards, carried them on for a number of years, and shipwrights came to live among them. But trade became slack and the employers wanted to reduce wages to 6/6 per day. The shipwrights said they could not live on that and would not. The masters said they could not afford to pay more than 6/6 per day. Hence there was a strike: and the question arises who is right? The alternatives are migration, or the giving up of shipbuilding work, or must discover that shipbuilding can be carried on at that price. [6]

The outcome of all this is that the labourer must get what he can by the produce of his labour. Now if the labourer lives in a place where the expenses are high, that affords no moral reason why his employer should pay him more.

Another question: whether the high price of commodities generally is a ground for high wages – but two cases there arise. Supposing that the price of all produce generally rises, is that any reason why the wages of the labourer should rise? If the high prices occur from a depression in gold, then I don't see why it should not extend at once to the rate of wages, or as soon as customs operating in the matter have time to alter: and I believe that is to a considerable extent the cause of the rise of wages in the present days. It is to a certain extent equal to a depression in the value of gold and so far the real wages of labour is not affected at all.

But supposing that the rise in price of some produce arises from the demand for that produce, will that be a ground of increase of the labourer's wages?

Read: Non-competing groups. Mill, Book II, ch. IV, ch. XI, next time ch. XIV.[7] Latter part of Theory, Chap. VIII.[8]

Other writers have considered wages in the mass. Senior makes that very sweeping assumption after pointing out that the earnings of the labourer may vary – that he may at one time earn £100, say, and after 20 years labour £10,000 with possibly less labour per day. Yet after allowing that he goes on to assume that the mass of labour may be considered as a kind of average.[9] Then political economists go on to explain what are the causes of the differences of wages and they generally

[6] For a full discussion of the effect of labour costs and other circumstances on the shipbuilding industry in nineteenth century London, see S. Pollard, 'The Decline of Shipbuilding on the Thames', *Economic History Review*, second series, 3 (1950–1) 72–89.

[7] These are the chapters 'Of Competition and Custom', 'Of Wages' and 'Of the Differences of Wages in Different Employments'.

[8] Entitled 'Concluding Remarks'. It was presumably the first two sections, 'The Doctrine of Population' and 'Relation of Wages and Profit', which Jevons wished his students to read in connection with this lecture.

[9] Senior, op. cit., p. 141.

adopt the views of Ad. Smith, [x ch. 1 Book.] Here he explains that the difference arises partly from the policy of nations which nowhere leaves things at perfect liberty; but partly from the circumstances of the employments themselves which . . . .* in the imaginations of men, make up the small gain of some to counterbalance the great gain of others.[10] In fact here the pecuniary aspect or the simple economical aspect of the subject breaks down and we find that the employments themselves are agreeable or disagreeable.

Then I will briefly enumerate the circumstances Smith took. 1st. Agreeableness or disagreeableness of employments. 2nd. Easiness or cheapness, or the difficulty and expenses of learning. 3rd. The constancy or inconstancy of employment. 4th. Small or great trust reposed in those who exercise it. 5th. The probability or improbability of success. Now there is no doubt that these circumstances do very much affect the rate of wages to be obtained and the illustrations are almost endless. You can take almost any trade and find that it is subject to these circumstances. e.g. clerical profession. What is the cause of the small salaries obtained by curates? Hope of interest: and then it is agreeable and connected with a social position: and altogether nothing disagreeable in the occupation. Then, it is a very easy occupation to learn, at any rate judging by the degrees that are passed by the generality of church curates, they don't get a high standard. And probability of success is very considerable – in fact almost certain.

Contrast civil service or various employments where there is nothing particularly agreeable in the employment, no great prizes, but sure to be supported through life if well behaved – and superannuation at the end. Now if a man under ordinary circumstances goes into the civil service he has little prospect of getting more than £500 or £600 per annum to the end of his life – for as a rule higher offices are not open to civil service. Therefore there we have absence of great prizes, but presence of certain moderate success. The pay of the civil service is probably higher than the pay of the clergy as a whole. For after all the clergymen who receive £1,000 a year or more are comparatively few. The barrister's profession is distinguished as the most uncertain of all: prizes greatest, to those peculiarly fitted, and proportion of failures greatest. The successful barrister has everything before him – an attractive career. But then, unfortunately, these large prizes are carried off by men of peculiar aptitude of good memory, and powerful intellect, and great powers of

---

* ?   (H. R.)

[10] What Rylett noted down here is a somewhat garbled version of the well-known passage in the *Wealth of Nations*, book 1, chapter x, which actually reads 'Partly from certain circumstances in the employments themselves, which, either really, or at least in the imaginations of men, make up for a small pecuniary gain in some, and counterbalance a great one in others'. This is followed, not preceded, by the statement about the policy of Europe. Cf. *Wealth of Nations*, 1, 101.

physical endurance. Good health is essential. In addition to these, and other peculiar qualities, in some branches of the profession – considerable oratory, judgment, tact and general knowledge. So that the number who combine all these favourable circumstances is comparatively few. A great proportion more obtain moderate success; very large number simply fail altogether as barristers and are drafted off into other professions – secretaries, etc. Sir James Paget[11] inquired into the case of 1,000 students. Their object was to become physicians or surgeons:

23 achieved distinguished success
66   „   considerable success
507   „   fair success
124   „   very limited success
720 or only 3 out of 4 continued in their profession
    and were more or less successful.
56 failed entirely
96 left the profession
87 died within 12 years of commencing practice
41 died during pupillage

This would seem to show that the proportion of failures is not very considerable. 276 didn't achieve what they wanted.

But there is one point overlooked by Smith, although it is important as determining the rate of remuneration, and that is the comparative abundance of suitable classes of men – and this is not met by any of Smith's remarks; but I may now refer to the mental and bodily characteristics by which men are brought up – =circumstances beyond their own control – unless it is met by the observation about easiness or expense of learning. E.g. for a man to become an iron puddler he must be able to endure standing before a hot furnace and turning the iron with a rod and accordingly the supply of men of that sort is limited: and again considerable skill is wanted; add to that that it is laborious and disagreeable work, and the result is that enormous wages are earned in a brisk state of trade. On the other hand certain classes of occupations, just the opposite, of no present necessity for peculiar talent or bodily qualification. Army e.g., a recruit must be of good health, must have a certain amount of muscular power – but still no particular strength is required. No education whatever is required: entrance examinations not required. In consequence, taken together with some disagreeable points about the matter, considered as a kind of last resort for those who are

---

[11] Sir James Paget (1814–99), distinguished surgeon, who in a paper delivered at St Bartholomew's Hospital gave the results of an inquiry into the careers of one thousand of his former students within fifteen years of their entering the hospital. Paget, 'Medical Students', *JRSS*, 32 (1869) 453–6.

unable to succeed in other things. Pay low but perfectly certain. Pension in the background – except in bad health. But difficulty now in getting recruits; either the pay will have to be raised or circumstances of the soldier have to be improved. The circumstances of other trades have risen and there is a general progress of comfort and wealth. Then again, other occupations. Now many little kinds of business that a man can take up: a man who has got out of line of some other business starts as a wine merchant or as a house agent. Consequently profits are small in some of these.

The general result is this, that there are two principal classes of circumstances governing differences of wages. 1st. The comparative abundance of men suitable for a trade, and secondly the comparative attraction of those trades for which a man is suitable. Generally a man's choice is a limited one. A man can only be attracted by comparative advantages of trade: so that there is competition on the part of professions. The principle of the subject then is this, that within a sphere of choice the aggregate attractions of the trades will tend to become equal. This is illustrated by taking the case of a soldier and policeman because physically speaking there is not much difference between them. The policeman is perhaps superior to the soldier. Other circumstances sufficiently similar to allow of most men choosing between them. Then what is it that makes the pay of a policeman higher than that of a soldier? A policeman's power is physical and mental – night work for the policeman has not the attraction of the lazy life of the soldier.

Profits
This is a subject closely related to the preceding, provided we strike out the element of pure interest. The Total Produce is divided into Rent + wages + profit. Profit is the remuneration of the employer, who is also called the entrepreneur – which we should translate into English – undertaker. The employer is the one who directs, and who bears the risk. He is sometimes a capitalist, but he may be sometimes risking the money capital of other people, which in the modern system of limited liability companies is becoming rather too common. But there must be somebody who combines capital, skill, labour & direction. The total remuneration of these is profit: but this is capable of analysis into

1st Pure interest on the money invested + remuneration of wages of the people who superintend the work + remuneration of risk or what we may call insurance + rent for peculiar advantages. I think there is that 4th element. But then with the exception of insurance these lead us back to the former formula respectively, so that we have as before, rent + wages + interest.

But we will leave interest just for the present.

Now, as to wages and superintendence we may repeat what we said as to labour. The labour of superintendence is labr. requiring mental skill and so on, but governed by much the same conditions as other labr. — i.e. by the number fit for this work and the agreeableness or disagreeableness of the work itself.

Rent with peculiar advantages arises from various circumstances. One way in which it arises is the reputation of a particular family or a particular name. The reputation of being wealthy and trustworthy is invaluable to a banker. Then the mere name of a person goes to infer that a man shall make a large profit, etc.* Then there is the reputation for business which is acquired by a long course of success and when once acquired maintains itself. Another, patent rights. The common sense of man would show that the man with large capital managed with skill must have greater success than those with lower. He can go into risky but probably profitable things in a way that others cannot. A man of large capital buys up shares and everybody buys. The shares go up in consequence and he sells out. If you look into Senior you will see he fully recognises these peculiar advantages are of the nature of Rent. As to wages of superintendence it simply resolves itself into ordinary . . . .[12] If a man is to live in the middle of the black country or in the middle of mountains, or has to go to the West Indies, etc., then he must receive extra remuneration as a general rule. Anybody with ordinary business ability that likes to go to China or Japan is sure to make a 1,000 a year.

Next time go to interest and risk: also conflict between capital and labr. Read Senior where he refers to this subject – latter part of his book.[13] Mill corresponding portions.[14]

LECTURE XII

TRADE UNIONS AND THE RELATIONS OF CAPITAL AND LABOUR

Jan. 28/76.

Trade Unions, some think, are a new thing and a rising danger, but they are quite as old as England, and appear at least 1,000 years ago, even supposing that one does not go back to the Saxon guilds. A kind of union or co-operation is innate in Saxon nature, and in the Saxon times there

* ?   (H. R.)

[12] The sentence ends here, without punctuation or explanation; Rylett presumably failed to take down the rest of the passage.

[13] Senior, op. cit., pp. 185–99.

[14] Mill, *Principles*, book II, chapter XV; book IV, chapter VII, pp. 400–15, 758–96.

were various kinds of guilds, peace guilds for religious and social purposes, and then again trade guilds. But there were early associations of foreign traders, especially those connected with Flanders, and one union of this sort long had a place called the Steelyard, which existed for centuries [Ethelred II].[1] These social and religious guilds more resembled the present friendly and benefit societies. They were distinctly recognised in the Saxon laws. But a kind of trade union which is more closely the same as those now existing was that of the Free Masons, which is also remarkable as existing now. The freemasons themselves date their existence from a very remote period – almost any time this side of the deluge if not before – but they really do, I believe, claim existence for something like 1,000 years.

The lodge in York is said to have existed in 926, and had a charter from Athelstan, and there is no doubt they existed throughout the middle ages, consisting strictly of a union of skilled masons engaged in building churches, cathedrals and abbeys. In 1425 an act was passed against chapters and masons because the good course and effect of the statutes of labourers were openly broken and violated by them. It was said this law could not be enforced agst. them. They continued for many centuries a trade union and in 1608 Sir Xtopher Wren was elected grandmaster on the ground of his skill as an architect. But in the 18th century the trade character was lost and there is no connection with building now. There are, however, some of the symbols of the origin – a trowel, mallet, etc.

Trade guilds appear to have existed for many centuries. One in Manchester is traced back to the year 856. During the middle ages these trade guilds and guilds of artisans became multiplied in all the towns of the kingdom, so that all the towns had a series of guilds representing the trades carried on. In later times they don't appear. L'pool perhaps had more. The organisatn. of these guilds was very simple. They all insisted on apprenticeship for seven years. Then apprentices became journeymen.

Subsequently they might become masters, but all the time ranks were under the supervision of the guild masters. A few years ago the statutes of some of these guilds were published in the volumes of the Early English Text Society.[2] They were minutely regulated by law. They became so

---

[1] The Steelyard was the London headquarters of Hanseatic merchants from the fourteenth to the sixteenth centuries. German merchants had settled in England as early as the twelfth century and there exist fragmentary references to foreign trade in the Anglo-Saxon period, including trade with Flanders during the reign of Ethelred II. See E. Lipson, *The Economic History of England*, 3 vols (1915; twelfth edition 1962) I, 512, 535–8, 581–2. Jevons appears to have based his account of medieval trade gilds partly on Lujo Brentano's *On the History and Development of gilds and the Origin of Trade Unions* (1870), originally published as an introductory essay to Toulmin Smith's *Ordinances of English gilds* (see below, n. 2), and which he recommends to readers of *The State in Relation to Labour* (1882) p. 90. Cf. Vol. V, Letter 595, n. 9, p. 42.

[2] *The original ordinances of more than one hundred early English Gilds: together with the old usages of the cite of Wynchestre; the ordinances of Worcester . . .* From *original manuscripts of the fourteenth and fifteenth centuries.*

well organized and powerful that at last in the reign of Elizabeth a law was passed regulating the duration of apprenticeships, i.e. giving the corporations or guilds actual legal power to monopolize their trades and to allow nobody to practise them without this apprenticeship. Thus throughout the kingdom each little trade in each little town became a close monopoly. This was directly contrary to the principles of the common law of England, which from the earliest times had upheld the freedom of labour—the sound principle that every freeman has a right to exercise his labr. in any way that is proper within the limits of the criminal laws, and judges have at all times held that nothing shall be allowed in restraint of trade, as it is called. The common law cannot stand against statute law. Common law is only immemorial custom, so this statute of Queen Elizabeth overturned the common law so far as it applied. Nothing could have been more agst. all principle and agst. the prosperity of the Kingdom, but fortunately the influence of the law was very much modified when the judges interpreted it as applying only to the trades and arts which existed when the law was passed. The law, in their opinion, had no prospective effect. Accordingly as some trades fell into disuse and others arose the influence of the law was interfered with.

During the 18th Century all these guilds became obsolete and gradually disappeared—with certain exceptions. For instance the London guilds, I suppose, being particularly rich, continued to exist and were recognised by law and they exist at the present day. But they are only corporations holding property for no definite purpose. It would be a good thing to overturn them all, and use their property for some useful purpose. When these guilds disappeared the manufacturing system rose—about, say, 1776. The object was to separate the master from the man. The men work together in factories, a large number under one master, instead of as in early times, when perhaps there was one master and two or three journeymen, and they all lived in the same house together. Then employed men began to consider their circumstances as opposed to their masters and to act in union and conspire, as it was then thought, to improve their position. The masters had no idea of allowing this sort of thing to go on, and being in possession of legislative power, they caused a series of acts to be passed, known as the combination laws, which prohibited any union of workmen for the purpose of raising wages or advocating any trade question. They were against the combinatn. of workmen in fact, and the conseqnce. was that this combinatn. of workmen assumed a great and violent character. The men were

Edited, with notes, by . . . Toulmin Smith . . . And a preliminary essay in five parts On the History and Development of Gilds, by L. Brentano (1870): no. 40 in the listed publications of the Early English Text Society.

determined to act in some way or other. Therefore not being allowed free and legal action, they broke out into riots every now and then and took to destroying machinery. The evil effects of these oppressive laws and the general policy of allowing men to form legal combinations was recognised in 1824 when the combination laws were repealed. It ceased to be illegal to form a society for the elevation of wages, and then it was the question of trade unions assumed something like its present shape – in fact so much like it that if you read any of the pamphlets written in 1832 you wd. think you were reading a pamphlet of the present day. All the questns. of strikes and piece work appear there exactly as they appear now so that at any rate we may trace unions back as far as 1830. But my own opinion is that we may trace them back to the beginning of the Saxon race. It is only the break out of the same tendency under different circs. There is an essential difference between trade unions and guilds, but only such a diffce. as might be expected by the change of circumstances.

There were no considerable changes in the law of trade unions, until a few years ago, when an act was passed allowing unions to be registered as friendly societies. The effect of that was to allow of incorporation in a certain form. The friendly societies acts gave legal status, gave the officers power to hold money and account to the society, which is not the case with an unregistered society. There can be no objection to this, and the only fault is that those funds wh. ought to be set aside are really at the mercy of the strike fund. There is no union where separate funds are separately invested. The union always asserts its power to use its money as it thinks fit. Accordingly in a great struggle the whole of the funds may disappear and the workmen who look forward to all those benefits are simply as good as defrauded out of them, except when they have gone into the union with their eyes open. Thus it was necessary that the unions should have almost unlimited power to make levies. Then as in the present state of this country most trades are growing and contain a large proportion of young men, the result is they don't find much difficulty in maintaining solvency. The minute superannuation fund shows how small a number have come on the society. In some way or other they have maintained their solvency. But these are not much worse than mere friendly societies: only one would prefer them to be assurance societies.

Regulation of hours and conditions of work. – So far as these are not intended to raise the rate of wages they appear to be most legitimate.[3] A man has a right to complain of what seems to him dangerous or unfair. Under the

---

[3] This confused passage in Rylett's notes reflects the theoretically valid but practically unrealistic view which Jevons consistently held that 'the rate of wages and the length of hours are two totally distinct things' and that 'when workmen want to lessen their hours of work, they ought not to ask the same wages for the day's work as before'. Cf. his 1868 paper 'Trades Societies: their Objects and Policy' reprinted in *Methods*, p. 107, *Primer of Political Economy*, p. 64.

factory system men certainly can have that system when they work in their own houses and no doubt one man who would insist upon going to work at eight instead of 6 or 7 wd. have small chance of carrying out his purpose; and united action seems legitimate when a number of men who join together in the same way –   –   . I wish they might take more rather than less. But all practically resolve themselves into:

1st. Regulation of wages – of course to raise a man's own rate of wages is a legitimate ambition; for everybody is more or less engaged in similar striving. The only question is as to the means employed in effecting it. And there the question subdivides very much. It might be put in this way. Is it possible by combination to raise wages? If so, under what circumstances? The third question is: Is it for the good of the country to allow such rise of wages?

Is it possible to raise wages? That turns upon the question, *From whom will come the increase of wages?* That is, no doubt, where men are misled. Because seeing their masters making considerable profits and paying them only a portion of the value of their produce they think that further demands will have to come out of the masters' pockets. In short they regard it as a question of labour *versus* capital. That is the common idea of the subject, and I am sorry to say that is what lends irritation to the matter – men regard masters as robbing them. But I shall go on to show that the state of the case is entirely different – that if they raise wages it does not come out of the masters' pockets – that their masters are those who can take care of themselves better than anybody else, that it comes out of the pockets of the consumers generally, and those who purchase the goods, and that these consumers generally include the whole working population of the country. It follows that supposing all trades to form unions, as the workmen themselves wish, that each trade will be benefiting itself at the expense of all other trades; that consequently there can be no considerable advantage to any workman whatever, and a very great disadvantage from the building up of insuperable obstacles between trade and trade. The only exception I can see to that is that capitalists are consumers when they spend a considerable amount of money in buildings, etc. – but that is different in character from the workmen's consumption. Therefore it seems to me that workmen's wages may be partly paid out of the excessive prices of articles of luxury. But at any rate it is as consumers they suffer, not as capitalists.[4]

So the trades unions, only a few years ago, were neither legal nor illegal. But since, it has been allowed that societies acting in restraint of trade, that is for raising wages, can legal [*sic*] exist. That act was passed by

[4] Cf. *The State in Relation to Labour*, pp. 101, 108.

Mr. Gladstone. [5] At the same time the act was passed inflicting penalties on any workman who should attempt to coerce other workmen on matters relating to work and trade. That is a totally different question. As long as a society is purely voluntary, it is not a monopoly. One thousand carpenters united and one not – then the latter is a free agent, – *if* union is really voluntary. We find that the object of the other laws concerning trade unions is to maintain them as perfectly voluntary as possible and penalties were enacted against workmen who injured or alarmed others. Then the argument of advocates of labour was that no special laws ought to be passed agst. workmen; that if they assaulted a workman, they should be punished for that; but that there shd. be no special crime created by law. I don't think that is a valid argument because one principle of legislation is that wherever there is a special temptation there ought to be a special enactment to prevent it. Most punishments are for special purposes. Forgeries for example. But a new act introducing the term master is merely a nominal change. To come to the actual modes of working we find there are three classes of purposes which they desire to carry out.

1st.   Regulation of wages.
2.   Regulation of Hours and modes of working.
3.   Their action as benefit societies.

This is their order of importance in the workman's eyes.

Of these three I begin with the last.

Nobody can hesitate to say that so far as they act as assurance societies they carry out the best object of civilisation, and no doubt in this way unions keep many off the rates. The amalgamated carpenters give 10/- for 12 weeks for no work; tool benefit to any amount; sick benefit 12/-per week for 26 weeks and 6/- afterwards; funeral benefit £12; accident benefit £100; superannuation benefit, 8/-, 7/-, 5/-; emigration £6 in addition to benevolent grants. These accounts show largest donations in sick benefit = £5,271; tools £524; sick £3,271; funerals £581; accidents £200; superannuation £16; trade privileges £1,818. Benevolence etc. £400. [6]

[5] Gladstone's Trade Union Act of 1871 gave legal status to unions, but was accompanied by a Criminal Law Amendment Act which attempted to protect public rights against union action. In consequence such activities as peaceful picketing were rendered illegal, and the trade unionists were antagonised. In fact, however, Disraeli had repealed this Act in 1875, replacing it by the Conspiracy and Protection of Property Act, which legalised peaceful picketing. See P. Magnus, *Gladstone* (1954) pp. 204–5, Ensor, *England, 1870–1914* (1936) pp. 132–3.

[6] For concise modern histories of the development of trade unions in Britain, see Henry Pelling, *A History of British Trade Unionism* (1963) and A. E. Musson, *Trade Union and Social History* (1974).

LECTURE XIII

CAPITAL AND LABOUR AS A WHOLE

The question is not so important as is usually supposed. It is only said that if unions gain more strength they will ruin the country by raising wages and producing foreign competition and in that way undermine the trade of the country. To a certain extent they do injure trade, e.g. by promoting emigration artificially; by opposing the introduction of machines to some trades especially to that of compositors, and most of all by prohibiting piece work. But these are breaking down. Machine made bricks, for example, are now allowed. Piece work is also progressing. My opinion is this that by degrees they (the unions) will become beneficial only when the same kind of fate overtakes them as has befallen the freemasons, and nothing more promotes that than the union of unions. So long as you have small local societies, secretly acting together, they assume the form of small clubs and conspiracies. But in the aggregate their action becomes more sensible. Their strikes are less numerous. They are beginning to find it impossible to enforce an equality of wages everywhere. In that way the wider a union becomes, and the more legal, the better. We find that the leaders of the unions are promising to establish a kind of absolute universal system of union including all the workmen of the country and more than that, an international society. [1] By this latter means everything was to be made happy all round – except for the capitalists. But when you carry such a system too far it acts against itself. You can raise wages for one trade or one place, but then you take the money out of one place or trade, and when you make it universal it is carried to an absurdity.

Now, as to the proposed modifications of the arrangements between employers and men, that is known under the name co-operation. Coöperation is one of those vague terms that means different things with every difft. person and it is distinctly applied to at least 3 difft. schemes. It came into very common use in connectn. with cooperative retail societies which exist all round the country and wh. commenced so far back as 1795. There is one still existing in Kingston on Hull of that date, and it has now about 4,000 members. But the rise of the system may be put down to 1832. It is more popularly known as dating from 1844, when the Rochdale pioneers was started, [2] the success of wh. led to a great extension

[1] See Julius Braunthal, *History of the International, 1864–1914*, translated by Henry Collins and Kenneth Mitchell (1966).

[2] The Rochdale Society of Equitable Pioneers, the most successful of the large number of co-operative retailing societies established in the first half of the nineteenth century, opened a small shop in 1844 on a capital of £28 raised by subscription among twenty-eight labourers. For a contemporary history, see George Jacob Holyoake, *The History of the Rochdale Pioneers* (1858); cf. also Jack Bailey, *The British Co-Operative Movement* (1955) pp. 17–18.

of the principle. These societies are not really unions of capitalists and workmen. They are simply organisations for the cheap retailing of ordinary commodities. They took their rise amongst working classes originally, but they have curiously enough spread to the wealthier classes in the form of civil service or supply associations. But they have but little connection with the subject of labour and capital and I will only say that they appear to save the expense of competition. The retailer has to make his way against another, but in one of these associations, there is no expense of advertising, because members are banded together, all bound to act as purchasers. The success of them may be regarded from two points of view. Do they succeed or should we expect them to succeed? we do find them to succeed, tho' there have been some serious breaks down. The civil service association is so prosperous that they don't know what to do with their profits. Taking it from the a priori point of view political economists entertain great doubts as to such a society succeeding, for want of the master's eye. I entertain doubts myself, especially in cases where the qualities of goods require delicate judgment and where the buying of these goods is a very responsible occupation – where bribes may be so easily brought in.[3]

The Mutual principle is not confined to supplying. The principle is this: that a number of people combine to carry on some kind of industrial occupation, and instead of paying the profits over to any separate body of capitalists they divide it among themselves ultimately. This mutual principle is brought into operation in insurance societies, which are of two kinds, those started for profits and those started by people to be insured. Ship insurance companies are generally mutual. Shipowners sometimes agree to insure each other and the whole of the profits is divided amongst themselves. Building societies also are usually on mutual principles. Now, the whole of these supply associations represent the same principle and it is a perfectly sound principle, on this condition, that you can get a managing body with an acting manager and a staff which can be made vigilant and active.[4]

The next form of cooperation is entirely different, namely, of cooperative protective companies. These are ordinary joint stock companies, simple limited companies, as they are called, but in wh. the capital is supplied by working men themselves, and thus men are their own shareholders. This is by no means a new thing. There is an account in

[3] The Civil Service Supply Association, the first middle-class co-operative, was founded in 1864 by a group of Post Office clerks who clubbed together to buy a chest of tea. The Association opened a retail shop in the Strand in 1868, at first dealing only in groceries, but by the 1870s the Association was able to cater for general household needs. See Alison Adburgham, *Shops and Shopping 1800–1914* (1964) p. 216.

[4] See Harold E. Raynes, *A History of British Insurance*, second edition (1964), p. 180; Barry Supple, *The Royal Exchange Assurance. A history of British Insurance, 1720–1970* (Cambridge, 1970) pp. 103–46.

Mill.[5] He enters into the subject pretty fully, going back to 1848, when the idea partly arose. But it has started up in various ways e.g. on the diggings in Australia. From 1854 to later than that it was quite common for companies of miners to be formed who were thus the miners and yet found all their own capital.[6] Quartz often done in this way. But more lately by degrees the principle has come into operatn. in many different places and forms and we have heard a good deal about these companies. Many have broken down sadly. Half a dozen in Manchester, some in Oldham, and in all these cases the word co-operation is excessively vague; and their remnants have been very small down to that small balance in the cooperative bank. In some cases it was an essential point that a large part of the profits should be given to the workmen as a bonus i.e. half the profits shd. be given to the workmen in proportion to wages and that only the other half shd. be given to them as capitalists = and that 5 per cent as capitalists and the remainder as bonus.* Such a scheme has the great advantage of stimulating each individual to exertion and vigilance, to keeping watch over his fellow workmen that they shall not unfairly scamp their work, and it is only where there is some provision of that sort that there is much advantage in this form. The mere dividing up the share capital into very small quantities wh. seems now to be called cooperation is rather a step in the wrong direction, because supposing these shares to be owned by people not working in the company, wh. is the case in Oldham, very often you have a number of people without sufficient motive to speed their labour in supervision of the work. There is this tendency even in great railway companies. I have never been at a railway meeting, but I am told they are a mere farce. What then may we expect in small companies. The probability is that the management falls into the hands of a few men who have their interests involved in some way. Then I believe the general extensn. of these so called co-operative companies is a very doubtful matter, unless the intelligence of the people be very much increased or unless the working men themselves are shareholders. If that can be carried out then you will have a really good state of things. But the workmen generally have not sufficient capital to manage the business and have to borrow or bring in capitalists from the outside.

The third form of cooperation is one that scarcely exists at the present day, viz. industrial partnerships, which is the truest form of cooperation to my mind. It is that where employers are the main capitalists, but where

---

[5] Mill, *Principles*, book IV, chapter VII, § 6, pp. 775–94.

[6] An unsuccessful attempt to form a miners' co-operative on the Australian goldfields was the Clunes Quartz Gold Mining Co., which consisted of one hundred miners who each contributed £15 for a share. See Geoffrey Blainey, *The Rush That Never Ended* (Melbourne, 1963) p. 67. Cf. Jevons's *Diary of a Visit to the Gold Diggings*, in Vol. I, appendix, pp. 213–38.

* ?   (H. R.)

they voluntarily consent to share part of the profits with the men. This is what might be called the bonus system perhaps, i.e. when a share of the profits is given over and above the ordinary wages for superior diligence and constancy of the workmen. You will find an account of some of the earlier partnerships of this kind in Mill, Leclaire in Paris; Paris and Orleans Railway Company.[7]

But in later times, in England, two or three attempts have been made. Briggs' collieries where the men were taken into counsel as well as gave money. Head & Co. formed a most complete and carefully considered scheme, the principal parts of which were that ten per cent of the profit was to be laid by as the masters' share in each year when there was as much as that. Anything beyond that was to be divided into two portions, one as extra profit to the masters and one half as bonus to the men. That was the principal point. Then there were a number of minor arrangements, e.g. during years when there was a small profit the masters were to have the profit up to 5 per cent and this 5 per ct. was to be the first claim upon the subsequent years profit wh. was perfectly fair, because the men always secured their wages, therefore the masters should secure their ordinary interest for the capital invested. There were provisions also for bad debts and another fund for depreciation. This carried on successfully for some years, and a considerable bonus, $2\frac{1}{2}$ per cent or more was paid. For some reason or other, however, the scheme was discontinued. The Briggs arrangement the Unions disturbed and must have done the same for Fox Head & Co.[8] I think the unions thought such arrangements would upset them. The point was could men be members of such partnerships and be members of a union too? If while giving a part of their profits to the men they were to be subject to strikes and have the wages raised at inconvenient times it would be almost impossible to carry on. But the system of bonus is spreading in a quiet manner. Merchants' clerks sometimes receive it, and banking clerks, too. The law now allows this to be done more freely than usually it did. Formerly those who received profits had to bear debts.

The great objectn. raised by employers to this system, i.e. that of publishing balance sheets, is that it reveals the state of their accounts, which in many trades would be inconvenient. In speculative trades profits are variable. This doesn't apply to companies who publish their balance sheets every year. In these cases, then why should not a share be

[7] Mill, *Principles*, book IV, chapter VII, § 5, pp. 769–75. There is no mention by Mill of the Paris and Orleans Railway Company's scheme, but see Jevons, *The State in Relation to Labour*, p. 143.

[8] The example given by Jevons of the coalowners Briggs, of Whitwood and Methley Collieries, Yorkshire, was also used by J. S. Mill – *Principles*, book IV, chapter VII, § 5, pp. 774–5. Their profit-sharing experiment was abandoned in 1875. The case of Fox, Head & Co. was familiar to Jevons, who had corresponded on it about a year earlier. See Letters 289, Vol. III, p. 165, and 382, Vol. IV, p. 51, and *The State in Relation to Labour*, pp. 141–6.

put apart for the workman? It wd. benefit everybody, and yet curiously enough I have not heard of any productive companies distributing a bonus.

Other remedies for doing away with the strife between capital and labr. – The remedy ought to be a radical one. But the differences are so numerous that some mere premise seems necessary. One form is that of some established tariff of wages carefully drawn up so that whenever the prices of goods vary wages shall be made to vary at the same time. That is especially applicable to the iron or coal trade where variation of prices is considerable and where such a large part of the prices goes in the form of wages. Altho' this has been proposed many times and has been attempted to be carried out I don't think it has ever succeeded. There is no doubt that the sliding scale arrangement is better than leaving it for bargain at the moment. It at any rate makes one bargain last for a length of time.

But you will easily see that it is not a thorough resolution of the matter, because the sliding scale cannot be maintained for any length of time. The changes which take place, the different rates of money and the prices of materials must greatly modify the comparative profits of the men and the masters, so that the tariff and scale would have to be revised now and then. It is a matter in wh. the free action of supply and demand ought properly to govern eveything.

Then the next form is simply that of arbitration. Questions are referred to certain men to be determined in a binding manner. An arbitrator is one who has power to fix. It very often succeeds. But difficulties arise and men often refuse to accept the decision given when it turns against them. Apart from this arbitration is only a makeshift. But there are no principles in the matter. It is simply a matter of bargain.

The third form is conciliation, a milder and sounder form of arbitration, the diffce. being that the award is not intended to be compulsory. The conciliator is a mere go-between; but being a trusted man is allowed to go through the books and receive the master's views and those of the men, and then endeavour to find some medium course. As a makeshift the solution is a very admirable one. It scarcely can do harm, but at the same time it is by no means always successful, and the attempts which have been made to effect a system of conciliation have broken down very much. An act of Parliament passed some years ago allowed every town in the country to form a society willing to undertake the consideration of the difficulties. A Board was appointed in Manchester by the Chamber of Commerce and it existed for some years, and then quietly dissolved themselves on the ground that no cases had ever been submitted to them. [9]

[9] An Act establishing Courts of Conciliation and Arbitration was passed in 1867, as a result of pressure from employers as well as trade unions from the 1850s. See Musson, op. cit., p. 28.

So that it does not seem that employers and employed were very desirous to conciliate.

The conclusion I should come to is simply this – that there is no absolute remedy for the troubles of capital and labour; that it is only a matter of bargain and the conflict of interests – however much you may try to mitigate these troubles you will not succeed – and that it is only in a gradual progress of affairs that any real amelioration will take place, and that will mainly consist in great progress of intelligence on the part of the men. I believe myself that the masters generally speaking are quite correct – and the newspapers on this subject are almost entirely – that free trade and free competition both of employers and workmen is the true thing and that both strikes and lock outs and all those violent measures are entirely wrong. The competition which takes place is that which takes place in domestic service – the servants taking the places where they are satisfied and leaving where they are not. And I believe that workmen will one day come to see that, and then unions will take the form of friendly societies.

––––––––––

"Value" next.

LECTURE XIV

VALUE

Feb. 11

We come now to value – the centre subject of political economy. When we began, the subject matter of the science was said to be Wealth: and the synonym of that is, what has value. Senior defines wealth thus: things which are transferable, limited in supply, productive of pleasure and preventive of pain. [1] If this is so, then we have a definition of what value is. But now we must go more carefully into the matter. The word value comes from the Latin through the French valour to be strong – and therefore means power or strength. But it is one of the most difficult and ambiguous words we have to deal with. Smith discriminated between value in use and value in exchange, and he remarked that the most difficult paradox of the whole subject was: things that have greatest value in use have often little or no value in exchange. I have no doubt that remark contains the fundamental difficulty in political economy, because

[1] See above, p. 9.

it shows that value in one sense can be founded upon use, upon value in use, or, what is the same, utility. Value in use is doubtless coincident in meaning with utility in one of its senses; but then utility as I shall show is vaguely used and it is because the word utility is so used that we have this paradox: but first of all I must distinguish and particularise the way in which we use the word value. Value in exchange means the proportion or ratio in wh. things are exchanged. Mill indeed speaks of value as meaning the general power of purchasing or as the command wh. its possession gives over purchasable commodities generally. [2] But I object to such an expression as general power of purchasing, as having no definable meaning whatever. There are thousands of different kinds of commodities, all varying in every particular, and unless you specify wh. of these you mean no definite idea attaches to the expression. Therefore – wherever you use the word value, you ought to have a clear notion of the two things wh. are exchanged the one for the other. The value of iron in copper is a definite idea, or the value of corn in iron. If two quarters of corn can be had for one ton of iron then we have the ratio of two to one. Therefore, for value, as often as possible, we will use ratio of exchange. The ratio of a ton of pig iron is nonsense – at any rate it clearly implies the existence of something else with wh. there must be a ratio. No doubt in ordinary discourse we are accustomed to take money or gold as the understood term of comparison. So that by the value of two quarters you would generally mean the ratio of exchange of corn for gold or price, so that price expresses ratio to the current legal tenders. But I don't think that people always bear this in mind. I believe that people commonly attach a certain definite absolute meaning to value – meaning the degree of estimation in which they put it for their own purposes very often. In short I believe the ambiguity of the word and the mixture of meaning with utility still exists, and therefore I think it so much better to use a definite expressn., viz. ratio of exchange, wh. can hardly be confused with utility. Then again there is another expression that shows the word to be curiously used. If I say the value of a ton of pig iron is £7, is that a perfectly correct expression? No, it should be the value of a ton of iron is equal to £7.

Mill says the value of a thing means of the quantity of some other thing that it exchanges for (Ch. VI 290 p.). [3] It shd. be the value of a thing means that it exchanges for some other thing in a certain ratio.

How values are governed. First it may be remarked that ratio or value, as he says, being a relative term there cannot be such a thing as a general rise in all values, for that would be about as absurd as everybody

[2] Mill, *Principles*, book III, chapter I, § 2, pp. 456–7.
[3] 'Value is a relative term. The value of a thing means the quantity of some other things, or of things in general, which it exchanges for.' – Mill, *Principles*, book III, chapter VI, § 1, p. 497.

growing corn for everybody else. That being obvious we come to the laws of supply and demand. They are the most important laws of the whole subject and they are phrases well known. It has long been recognised that in some way or other the values of things depend on the relative activity of supply and demand; but the words themselves have been used with great vagueness and uncertainty. In fact, each word supply and demand has a double meaning probably: viz: intensity of mental feeling which actuates the holders or the purchasers of goods, and secondly the quantities of goods they offer or demand. It does not follow that the mental feeling is in exact correspondence with the quantity. For example a person may have an exceedingly active demand for, say, tobacco, but he may have none of it at all and may not have any means of getting it. Then his active demand is without effect upon the price of tobacco. Or, again, a man might have a large quantity of pictures of an artist, but at the same time he might have such a vivid pleasure in possessing them that he would not allow them to go from him. In that case they are not supplied – they are not offered on the market. Accordingly the definite idea first to be attached to supply and demand is that they are quantities, not mental states. At present the quantity offered and quantity supplied are the facts of importance, but observe that these facts will entirely depend in many cases upon the prevailing ratio of exchange. On the one hand you may perceive so much offered for certain goods that no owner of any sense would refuse. You do hear of people saying that they wd. not part with a thing for a certain price, but of course there are few people who wd. not part for a good price. Then the general principle is this, that if the price offered is sufficient the whole of the commodity will become supply or more generally speaking the higher the price the greater the supply. On the other hand we can easily conceive that price, i.e. ratio of exchange, may be so low that nobody would wish to part with what they have. In the case of many commodities like corn and useful clothes, etc., if they cannot be used now they can in the course of the next few years. There is an exception to that of course in the case of perishable things. Herrings, for example, may exceed your power of consumption. Then the ratio of exchange may fall in almost any degree because when they cannot be preserved they have very little utility. Accordingly, the simple formula of the law of supply and demand is simply this: the lower the value or ratio of exchange, the greater the demand; the higher the value the less the demand.

Value	*Supply*	*Demand*
higher	greater	less
lower	less	greater

The whole problem of value is supposed to be summed up in this equation, that the value will be adjusted to that point at which the quantity demanded is equal to the quantity offered. But Mill says that this is analogous to an equation.* It had been previously said that the law of supply and demand depended on a ratio, that it was the ratio between supply and demand. He said the proper mathematical analogy was an equation:[4] but he should have said that it was an equation and not merely an analogy. As to how this equation is settled it is difficult to express except the higgling of the market decides it as Adam Smith says.[5] But it is perfectly well known how the prices of things are determined in any large market. The general rule is this: that any large purchases raise the prices. Small purchases lessen the prices. Large supplies lessen the prices; shortness of supplies raise the prices. That is only another expression of the laws of supply and demand, but the way it works up is this, that if anybody goes to market, brings a quantity of goods and tries to get them sold at the current price and cannot, then he is tempted to under-sell the others. Now if this holder really finds toward the end of the market that he cannot get rid of it, and has to do so, he lowers his price, and the fact is that the other sellers must lower their prices. There is such a thing as selling under the market price where it may not affect the market directly. Generally, however, sales are known and the effect is known. Then in purchasing if a man wants certain goods and cannot find anybody to sell at the price he has to pay more and the others get to know and raise their prices.

One important principle is this, that *in the same market there cannot be two prices for the same kind of goods at the same time*. The price may vary within five minutes. Again of course it may vary with any slight change in the quality of the goods. Then agn. the price need not be the same unless there is what we call a perfect market. Now if you endeavour to define what market means, it is this, that the market is any set of traders in an article who have information of the transactions which are going on, the probable supply and demand at the time, and the ruling price. In short a man is on the market when he knows what is going on in the market and in proportion to what he knows. If he is away for ten minutes he may be off the market. In short the market is constituted by the extent of information. That shows clearly how the higgling affects the quantity or price.

* ?   (H. R.)

[4] 'Thus we see that the idea of a *ratio*, as between demand and supply, is out of place, and has no concern in the matter; the proper mathematical analogy is that of an *equation*'. – Mill, *Principles*, book III, chapter II, § 4, p. 467.

[5] *Wealth of Nations*, book I, chapter V, contains a reference to 'the higgling and bargaining of the market', but in reference to the relation between different grades of labour: I, 33.

How the state of prices is ultimately ruled. The doctrine of Mill, adopted from Ricardo, is that some things are governed in their value by supply and demand only, but that other things are not. There are many things which cannot be altered in the quantity of supply, things which Mill would say possessed monopoly value, namely, the pictures or books of a deceased person i.e. painter or author. Antiquities and curiosities of a certain kind. Certain substances are in continuous supply, the wines of a particular vineyard which is limited in extent.[6] Certain minerals are absolutely limited – one peculiar case is that of black lead obtained from Borodale. Antiquities not so limited in supply is the folio edition of Shakespeare's works. Then in this case Mill and Ricardo would maintain that the laws of supply and demand absolutely govern this. How is it that these rare things command such high prices? How is that in accordance with the law of supply and demand? It is *effective demand*, i.e. demand accompanied by the power to purchase. Many might demand this "Shakespeare's works" but not have the money to buy. Effective demand however must be looked forward to. But I believe it would be more correct to say that the demand for these pictures is the large sum of money that people are willing to give for them. It is the money that is the demand.

Mill distinguishes three classes of commodities. Those which are absolutely limited in supply, such as those already mentioned. Those wh. can be increased in almost any degree, but with increasing difficulty; and those of wh. the supply can be increased in any degree.[7]

Now as regards the second and third classes these writers hold that a different principle comes into operatn. and that values are governed by cost of production. Then we get into this very doubtful and troublesome talk about the cost of production. But I ought first to explain that in such cases there are really two values existing or supposed to exist, viz. the market value and the natural or cost value: altho' it is said that things are govd. by the cost of production, yet they never are exactly govd. by it. The market value is always above or below the actual or cost value, so that all you can say is that there is a tendency for them to coincide. But if so the law of supply and demand intervenes very plainly. In short they allow that this law governs market values. The way in which it operates is

[6] Cf. Ricardo, *Principles*, edited by P. Sraffa, p. 12; Mill, *Principles*, book III, chapter II, § 2. The actual words employed by Mill were – 'There are things of which it is physically impossible to increase the quantity beyond certain narrow limits. Such are those wines which can be grown only in peculiar circumstances of soil, climate, and exposure.' Rylett's notes display some confusion here; it seems possible that they are an incomplete record of a passage in which Jevons distinguished between commodities such as the folio edition of Shakespeare which are in absolutely fixed supply, and others such as the product of a particular vineyard of which a continuing but limited supply could be produced.

[7] Mill, loc. cit., pp. 464–5.

well known. The chief cause is that things cannot be made instantaneously. They require some time to grow, or to be manufactured. Then as we saw in the case of wages, capitalists must undertake the procuring of things before the consumers need them: but the capitalists can estimate exactly how much will be wanted. Then again the supplies of raw materials depend so much upon the harvest and the course of the weather – so that speculators and others cannot definitely know how much they ought to keep on hand. This is the whole topic of the market reports that we see in newspapers. This all means that the laws of supply and demand really govern the market price and nobody can doubt it for a moment. But then in that case what becomes of this cost value, that is said to be a permanent or average, or natural rate? It is defined by this circumstance, that it just obeys the ordinary rate of wages and profit. Things are exchanged at their natural value when people can go on producing and selling them at those values. Cost of product = wages and profit of capital for the most part + taxes and what it calls the scarcity value of some of the raw materials also add an occasional element. The cost price is the price at which a thing can be produced with the ordinary rate of profit and the market price is whatever can be obtained above or below that.

Book III in Mill.[8]

LECTURE XV

HOW VALUE MAY BE SHOWN TO BE REALLY FOUNDED ON UTILITY

Friday, Feb. 17/75.

There is a distinctn. between value in use and value in exchange. Value in use = utility. But then utility is really used very loosely. It is generally used as referring to the ensemble of the qualities which make a thing of use to people generally. Gold is said to be useful because it is valuable, indestructible metal etc., and these qualities are supposed to make its utility. But then it is not useful if buried at the bottom of a mine beyond reach or divided into small particles so that it cannot be collected. In short gold is only useful when capable of being used. So a thing is useful when in a certain relatn. to the people wanting it. But if that be a correct description of utility then we have to distinguish between the whole utility which a thing can be to a person or utility of separate portions of it.

---

[8] Mill, *Principles*, book III, 'Exchange', pp. 455–701.

Now the degree of utility of any commodity means the utility of the last portion wh. has come into use. Taking any such common article as bread it would ordinarily be said that bread was an exceedingly useful thing. But the question arises is all bread or corn very useful, and I think the answer must be that it is not – that it is only when you have not enough of anything that you want more. Now suppose you have enough, you don't want more; then if more comes and you can't use it, it follows that you don't want it. Many things therefore are not useful. Thus in the Western States of America corn in time of a plentiful harvest is a drug. Then nothing is more unquestionably useful or valuable than meat, but on the plains of America meat is valueless and useless.

Then we may illustrate the utility of any ordinary article of that sort by a curve. In the case of bread you may conceive a certain number of pounds per day as consumed. Then the 1st. lb. per day sustains life and is infinitely useful. 2nd also useful as giving a moderate sustenance, 3rd. lb. hardly any use. 4th lb. no use at all because a man can't use it. 5th lb. would have hardly any value at all – except to give to the chickens.

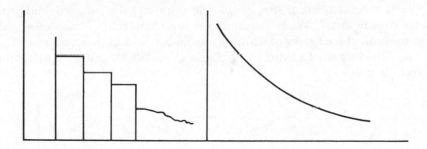

Then the height of a line in any portion of this curve = amount of utility. Smith almost falls upon the idea. He remarks that the desire for food is limited in every man by the narrow capacity of the human stomach: but it seems extraordinary that it should not have occurred to him, if limited then food is not all useful. He goes on to remark that the desire of convenience luxuries etc. seems to have no limit or certain boundary.[1]

Now we shall see how this theory of utility will lead to a theory of value, and that we may do so we must consider the position of two commodities.

Imagine two men shut up in prison and supplied with certain amounts of different kinds of food. The one has plenty of bread and the other plenty of meat.

[1] Smith, *Wealth of Nations*, book I, chapter XI; I, 165.

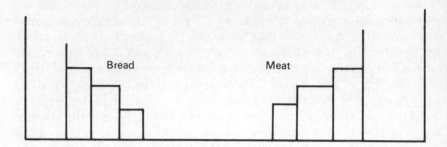

But usually we eat both bread and meat and the one would exchange with the other no doubt. Suppose the one were to give the fourth portion of his meat for the fourth portion of the other's bread: so that the fourth part of the one wd. be about equal to the first part of his own bread or meat respectively. Will they wish to exchange more? If so what are the determining circumstances. Suppose we try whether the exchange of this second portion would be profitable. It would be this: that the utility of a second portion wd. be more to him than what he has to part with. So that at that second portion they would be both equally satisfied and wd. exchange no more. We have, therefore, this result that exchanges would go on until the degrees of utility are equalised on both sides.

But dividing the quantities into portions is artificial and we must again resort to a curve:

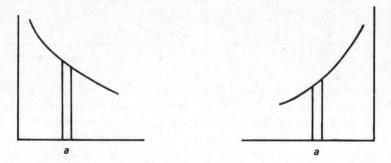

Now the line "a" represents the degree of utility of a small portion. Now when they cease exchanging, the utility of one small portion ought to be exactly equal to that of the other small portion.

We thus have a part of the law of exchange, namely that the degree of utility of bread multiplied by the small quantity given = the degree of utility of meat multiplied by the small quantity received. And when the man on this side finds that this is true and that to exchange any further portion wd. be to his loss he wd. exchange no more: or suppose that *a* equals amount of bread that A originally had and *x* equal quantity which he gives; then let *b* equal the quantity of meat B originally had and *y* = quantity he gives, then *y* = *x*.

ϕ expresses that combination of the *y* and *x*. ϕ *a* − *x* = the degree of utility of bread. Observe it is the degree of utility as it were of the last portion − that wh. remains when you get to the point *y* = *x*.

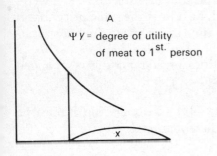

A

Ψ *y* = degree of utility of meat to 1ˢᵗ· person

x

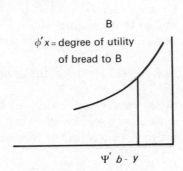

B

ϕ' *x* = degree of utility of bread to B

Ψ' *b* - *y*

Then the small quantity may be so expressed by the differential calculus

$$d\,x \qquad d\,y$$

So we get, A. $\phi(a-x) \times dx = \psi y \times dy$

and B. $\psi'(b-y) \times dy = \phi'x \times dx$

or $\dfrac{\phi(a-x)}{\psi y} = \dfrac{dy}{dx}$

Here we have the small quantity of bread or meat −

a in $\dfrac{\phi a - x}{\psi y}$ the degree of utility. So we may say that when the exchange terminates the degrees of utility are inversely as the small quantities last exchanged. It is curious that the result we arrive at is perhaps the most familiar mechanical principle that exists.

Now one more step, viz that the same commodity always sells at the same price in the same market, or the ratios of the exchange are always the same.

The whole quantities given and received are *x* and *y*. Not only *dy* and *dx* these are the last portions only. The result is that *y* by *x* must be half the same ratio of *dydx*² that there is the same ratio between all portions or

---

² This should obviously read $\dfrac{y}{x} = \dfrac{dy}{dx}$. From the ensuing sentence it seems possible that Jevons's actual words were '*y* by *x* must have the same ratio as *dy* by *dx*' and that Rylett misheard this.

commodities exchanged. This is perhaps not always true. It is not really true if sales take place in succession one after another. A great holder of some quantity who was going to have an enormous quantity of corn would begin selling it. His first sale and perhaps the second and third would be at the regular rate; but supposing he kept on, the lower the market would become, and in that way he might run down the prices. But that is not the question here, because these sales are not successive. Here we are looking at exchange which takes place at the same time, as it were, and in that case the whole quantity wd. be sold at the same price. But if that be true we can simply alter the equation and come to this final result,

that $\dfrac{\phi(a-x)}{\psi y} = \dfrac{y}{x}$ or the whole quantities of commodities exchanged

are inversely as the degrees of utility.

But here we are speaking only of A, who is satisfied: but B must be satisfied – then that is represented in the equation:

$$\frac{\phi' x}{\psi'(b-y)} = \frac{y}{x}$$

But does it necessarily happen that they are both satisfied? No. Both equatns. wd. have to be true before they were both satisfied. For one, if unsatisfied, wd. give a little more and so induce the other to exchange. The only objection to be raised against this is, unfortunately, that we don't know anything about what ϕ and ψ are. It is true that P. Economists talk about the law of supply and demand. They don't know what the laws are, and it is objected that to follow this way is to make economy mathematical and precise when there is nothing precise. To those who

view $\dfrac{y}{x}$ in the right way it does not mean anything more than that

as the price varies the demand varies. The unfortunate point is the exact determination of these quantities is almost impossible, and at present is practically impossible. But that is merely because of the perplexity of the subject and the want of data. Supposing we attempted to ascertain what is the degree of utility of bread, we could do this if nobody else did anything else with bread than we did* – but we don't know that. The difficulty is that some substances may replace others. Oatmeal, barley bread and pudding and so on take the place of bread, and potatoes are a very annoying substitute for you never can find how much the potatoes interfere. And then it would not be sufficient to know how much bread there is in the country. The only chance would be to lump kinds of food together – but equal weights are not equally nutritious.

* ? (H. R.)

Therefore we are thrown back upon various conjectures that have been made. Nobody denies that as the supply of corn runs short the prices of it rise very much. Now so slight has been the progress of inquiry in these subjects since the 17th century that we are obliged to go back to Fred[*sic*] King, who wrote in the latter part of the 17th century[3] before we get any estimate of the proportions between quantity of corn and ratio of exchange. I think it is disgraceful in the present state of science that the vague suggestion of an old fellow in the 17th centy. should be the only data we have of the dependence of our main supply of food on the demand. Yet he has to tell us that a defect of $\frac{1}{10}$ in the harvest will

raise the price $\frac{3}{10}$, a defect of $\frac{2}{10}$ will raise it $\frac{8}{10}$

$$\text{of } \frac{3}{10} \quad \text{''} \quad \text{''} \quad \text{''} \quad 1\frac{6}{10}$$

$$\text{of } \frac{4}{10} \quad \text{''} \quad \text{''} \quad \text{''} \quad 2\frac{8}{10}$$

$$\text{of } \frac{5}{10} \quad \text{''} \quad \text{''} \quad \text{''} \quad 4\frac{5}{10} \text{[4]}$$

This statement has been quoted over and over again. It is to be found in almost every book on Political Economy that touches on this subject. Say says this is probably exceedingly accurate.[5]

More specifically stated you come to this conclusion; that the price of corn varies inversely as the square of a certain quantity which may be stated with sufficient accuracy $\frac{5}{6(x-\frac{1}{8})^2}$. That represents the price where x is the harvest (its usual average amount) . So that if x should be reduced to $\frac{1}{8}$ part of the usual harvest the value of the corn would be infinite.

[3] Gregory King (1648–1712), herald, public servant, described by Jevons as 'one of the fathers of statistical science in England'. The figures quoted by Jevons form part of King's treatise *Natural and Political Observations and Conclusions upon the State and Condition of England* (1696). Charles Davenant based his *Essay upon the Probable Methods of making a People gainers in the Ballance of Trade* (1699) on King's treatise, but the work itself was not published until over a century later, when it was included at the end of George Chalmers's *An Estimate of the Comparative Strength of Britain during the Present and Four Preceding Reigns . . . A new edition, corrected and continued to 1801. To which is now annexed Gregory King's celebrated State of England . . . (1802).* See *T.P.E.*, fourth edition pp. 154–8.

[4] Jevons quotes as the source of this table Davenant's *Essay*, published in *The Political and Commercial Works of that celebrated writer Charles D'Avenant . . . relating to the trade and revenue of England . . . Collected and revised by Sir Charles Whitworth . . .*, 5 vols (1771) II, 226. See *T.P.E.*, fourth edition, loc. cit.

[5] No such precise reference to Gregory King's calculations appears to have been made in either of J. B. Say's principal works.

LECTURE XVI

SUPPLY, COST AND DISUTILITY

Feb. 25/76.

What we have said does not exclude the dependence of value on supply and demand. In short the utility of what is last received depends on the quantity supplied. Thus the theory I gave last time is in accordance with supply and demand. There arises the question how value depends on the cost of the productn. of articles or what is the relation between value and labour? There has been much discussion on this subject from Smith down to the present time. Smith thought labour was the best measure of value, because "labour is the natural price which we give for everything: all products are the products of labour and may be considered as exchanged for labour";[1] therefore he thought that the quantities of labour embodied in goods represented their value more nearly than anything else. That, however, entirely breaks down when we come to apply it, for several reasons, – at any rate *two* reasons. 1st. That labour is exerted in circumstances more or less advantageous; second that a man cultivating first class land produces two or three times as much corn as one cultivating sterile land at the top of the hill. There we get into a difficulty. The labour cannot possibly be the value there, because the corn that is produced is all of equal value.

A second objection is that labour itself differs in value exceedingly. It is one of the most variable things that exists, not only because different men have difft. muscular power; but because they have difft. skill and mental powers, so that whereas one man only earns £20 per year another earns £10,000. So that it would be much more true to say that the products of a man's labour are the measure of that labr. than vice versa. Take the case of a farmer. Suppose a farmer so experienced in the management of farms that he could make his farm yield £10,000 a year more than other people's farms. Then his knowledge and experience produce £10,000. The labourers are paid the ordinary rate of wages, i.e. what they wd. earn under ordinary management so it is clear that the directing farmer's skill is worth £10,000 a year. Thus we cannot suppose that labour is the measure of value.

Another most misleading statement is that labr. is the cause of value, or that it is only things upon which labr. has been expended that have value. I cannot imagine a more unfortunate error than this by Prof. Rogers in his Manual of Political Economy. At Chap. II page 7 he says "All objects

---

[1] *Wealth of Nations*, book I, chapter v. The passage given in inverted commas in Rylett's text is not an exact quote, but a rough paraphrase of the second paragraph of this chapter. Cf. above, p. 19, n. 2.

and services possessing value in exchange derive this value from the fact that labour has been expended on them. To this rule there is only one exception, i.e. land in fully settled countries. The aggregate amount of labour expended is the cause of the value attaching to the thing."[2] Now, if we are to attribute any consistent sense to this it must be that the value is more or less proportionate to the labour. He would mean that wherever labour has been expended value arises, and where not value will not arise: and that is contradicted by the very simplest facts. In the first place you may expend any amount of labour without creating value – Bessemer Ship,[3] Gt. Eastern, [4] Thames Tunnel.[5] Observe, in these, that there is no proportion whatever between the amount of labour and the result – that depends entirely on the skill which is applied, or the fortunate circumstances. The case of the harvest: the labr. applied in sowing and reaping and in preparing the ground in one year is twice as much as in another year.

Then, returning to Rogers, I have shown that where labour has been given value is not necessarily produced.

Then value arises where hardly any labr. has been applied at all – nugget of gold, for instance – (first discovery made by Shepherd who saw it sticking out.)[6] Supply of water, etc. e.g. a stream of water running thro' a man's land. Value arises with these without labour.

How it is that values are ultimately regulated by quantities of labour, or adjusted in relation to them, and the point of the whole thing is this, that it will not be every portion of a commodity which acquires value because of its cost of labour: but it will be new portions of the same commodity which will have value because they cost labour. In short, you have to distinguish the difference of price of different additions of the same commodity. To return to nuggets. I altogether deny that each portion of gold is valuable because it has cost labour; but it is nevertheless true that if you want some more gold you must, as a general rule, give an

[2] J. E. Thorold Rogers, *A Manual of Political Economy for Schools and Colleges,* published in the Clarendon Press Series (1868), second edition (1869).

[3] 'The Bessemer Saloon Steamship' was a vessel specially designed for the Dover – Calais route, incorporating a device patented by Sir Henry Bessemer in 1869 – a 'swivelling saloon' on hydraulic mounts which was intended to maintain a level position however much the steamer itself might roll.

On two trial runs, the last of which took place on 8 May 1875, the vessel proved very slow and failed to respond to her helm when entering Calais harbour, causing considerable damage to herself and the pier. As a result, all prospect of commercial success evaporated and the company sponsoring the venture was forced into liquidation, Bessemer protesting that its failure was in no way the result of his invention. See *Sir Henry Bessemer, F.R.S. an Autobiography* (1905) pp. 304–26.

[4] I. K. Brunel's last project, the 12,000-ton steamship, which at this date was being used as a cable – layer. See L. T. C. Rolt, *Isambard Kingdom Brunel: a biography* (1958) pp. 238–308.

[5] See Vol. I, p. 91, n. 2.

[6] Traditionally the beginning of the Australian gold rush dates from the accidental discovery by an aboriginal shepherd of a rock containing over 1200 ounces of gold, in July 1851. See Blainey, op. cit., p. 26.

amount of labour for it corresponding to its value – simply for the reason that you cannot pick up nuggets whenever you like. Observe, that if it were quite a common thing to pick up nuggets, gold would not have much value, so that the value of gold really arises from the fact that people cannot get as much gold as they like without labour. Thus it is the labr. spent upon the last addns. of gold which determine its value, or, in other words, the portions of gold got under the least favourable circumstances; or it is the cost of the most costly portion which gives value. Now, that avoids the difficulty of the nugget. The nugget when found is as valuable as the most valuable part, because one commodity cannot have two values in the same market. So it is the most costly portion which gives the value of the rest. Put into mathematical formula it is this: the degree of labour will be the painfulness of labour. l=labour; dl=small portion of labr.; u=utility; du=small portion of u. x=commodity; dx small portion of x. t=time.

The painfulness of labr. $= \dfrac{dl}{dt}$ or labr. in comparison with the time.

Then we have the productiveness of labr. wh. means the proportion of what is produced and the time in which it is produced, i.e. $\dfrac{dx}{dt}$

But we must also take into account the utility of that wh. is produced, because if you produce more of a commodity, that new addn. is not necessarily as valuable as the last portion, so that we have to introduce the degree of the utility wh. is $\dfrac{du}{dx}$. So that we come to this, that the degree of utility produced by a certain amt. of labour is $\dfrac{du}{dx} + \dfrac{dx^7}{dt}$.

Then the next question is when will labr. repay itself. How will you express the point at which labour ceases to repay itself. If you expend more labour you produce more commodity, and if you went on producing more and more we should have more than we want and then the degree of utility would sink. At what point then will you stop in the production of commodity? That commodity or labr. will be spent until the commodity produced agrees with the following result, viz that $\dfrac{dl}{dt} = \dfrac{dx}{dt}$ or the degree of painfulness of labr. is equal to the degree

---

[7] $\dfrac{du}{dx} + \dfrac{dx}{dt}$ should be $\dfrac{du}{dx} \cdot \dfrac{dx}{dt}$

Cf. *T.P.E.*, p. 176. Rylett wrote '$\dfrac{\partial l}{\partial t}$' and '$\dfrac{\partial x}{\partial t}$', but Jevons would not have used this notation.

of productiveness; – to the labr. multiplied by the degree of utility of the commodity produced.

But what we have next to do is to observe how this applies where more than the commodity is in use: for this applies to only one commodity.

It is apparent that if a man expends labour in producing two difft. commodities he will distribute them in such a way that the last portion of labr. spent will produce the same utility because if he did not do so there wd. be more advantage in distributing the labr. in other ways. Consider such a case as the production of corn and beef. Suppose a certain amount of labr. on each.*[8] If the last portion spent on corn wd. have produced more utility if spent on beef it ought to have been so spent. Therefore we come to this result that when labour spent in producing two quantities is exactly proportional, the utility produced in the two ways ought to be equal to each other. That may be expressed by an equation. If you suppose we are speaking of equal times (the amount of time spent upon the labour) it wd. be by taking $\dfrac{du}{dx} \cdot \dfrac{dx}{dt} = \dfrac{du^2}{dx} \cdot \dfrac{dx}{dt}$. But instead of taking "t" for time, in the book (Theory) I have taken l or quantity of labr. so that I shd. prefer to keep it similar to the book in this way.

$$\frac{du}{dx} + \frac{dx}{dl} = \frac{du^2}{dy} \times \frac{dy}{dl}\,^{9}$$

That expresses the fact that when the labour is proportioned properly between two commodities, the proportion of labour spent on corn produces the same amt. of utility as the same amt. of labour spent of beef, beef being y corn x.*

Now we come to connect these with the theory of utility and value, because the quantities exchanged are inversely as the degrees of utility.

The result is that there is a possibility of exchanging two commodities for each other and also producing them. Labr. will be expended upon each up to such a point that the degrees of utility are inversely proportional to the degrees of productiveness, while the ratio (or quantities exchanged) of exchange is in direct proportion to the degree of productiveness.

---

* ? (H. R.)

[8] 'and beef' is crossed out here and 'on each' written above it. The query may have related to 'and beef'.

[9] The equation is here given as it appears in Rylett's notes. The correct version appears in *T.P.E.*, p. 184:

$$\frac{du_1}{dx} \cdot \frac{dx}{dl_1} = \frac{du_2}{dy} \cdot \frac{dy}{dl_2}$$

* ? (H. R.)

Read the Chap. on Labr. in the Theory.[10]

Theme. Are pearls valuable because people have to dive to the bottom of the sea for them, or do people dive for them because they are valuable?

Next: Pass to "Money".

LECTURE XVII

MONEY

Friday, March 3/76.

Practically we measure value in money. Altho' not accurately, yet practically it is the form of expression commonly adopted. And again it is money which introduces perplexity into the subject so much and mystifies it. But I need not go much into the matter. I will ask you to read most of the work on Money.

Exchange is barter wh. consists in the direct exchange of two commodities each employed for useful purposes, apart from exchange, whereas *Money* is some commodity set apart for the purpose of facilitating exchange – lubricating the action as it were – just as oil is used in machinery. The principal point is to observe however that the money really serves many different purposes, 3 or 4 at the very least and in that way meets different disadvantages of barter. The first use of money is as a medium of exchange, i.e. it intervenes so that a person wanting to sell an article and to purchase some other article for it uses the money as the medium, i.e. to get over the difficulty of finding the two people who exactly want the possessions each of the other. e.g. purchase of houses. Connected with that is the diffty. of subdivision of values. Smith makes a great deal of the difficulty of division.[1] But money serves to subdivide as a medium of exchange. Next it serves as a measure of value. This usually given as the second use of money. It may serve as the measure and expression of value even when not used as a medium. In all the large transactions of England at the present day money is not needed because things are really written off or exchanged against each other in a complicated way. Nevertheless all the values are estimated and accounts are settled in terms of money. The purpose of this measure of value is to

[10] *T.P.E.*, chapter v. The theme given by Jevons is based on the well-known statement by Whately, *Introductory Lectures*, second edition (1832), Lecture ix, pp. 252–3.

[1] Smith, *Wealth of Nations*, book i, chapter iv,i, 24–31.

simplify and to define values in a clear manner, because without it we should have to think of each commodity in terms of various other commodities – prices would assume a most complicated form. You would have no ideas of quantity of value at all; you wd. have not here a clear idea of quantity of value than you have now of quantity of utility. Quantity of utility cannot be put into figures because we have this common measure – money.

The common measure might vary from year to year, or even from month to month, without making any serious harm, provided that all the expressions of prices varied accordingly. All the ratios wd. remain the same. But it is quite different when you come to a *third* use of money, i.e. as a standard of value from time to time. Tho' we might do without a measure of value we could not do without a standard of value and that is a difficult question. Indeed, the subject of a standard of value is a very difficult one. It has never been thoroughly solved and the secret of the difficulty is this – *that it ought not to be a standard of value, but a standard of utility.* You remember that the word value was merely a relative term = ratio between two commodities. Now, when people talk of a standard of value, they want some means of getting back at a future date the same value that they give at the present time. It is used with respect to debts of long standing. Now what people want is to be sure that they get back at a future time what is valuable to them. But, then, value there really means utility, because what people want ultimately is command over conveniences and luxuries. Now as I have said there is no real way of measuring and defining utility, and the only approximation we can make to a standard of value is something which shall exchange for other articles, on the average, in as nearly an unchanged rate as possible. But in order to give any meaning to that you must define the mode in wh. you take your average. And altogether the question is one of great difficulty. We shall probably return to the subject of the standard of value, but, now, I remark that practically it is money that is used as the standard of value and for the payment of debts. Leases of any length are made in gold money. But there is no possible reason why all such future payments should not be stipulated for in coal – so many tons of good coal would be the best terms upon which you could get your lease, i.e. as receiver, not as payer.

Then a 4th purpose to wh. money is practically applied is that of a *store of value,* i.e. a form in wh. you may condense your wealth, convey it away, or hide it or keep it for future contingencies. Mr. Gladstone makes the interesting remark that in the time of Homer gold was used as a store of value and not as a medium of exchange. [2] It is remarkable that in the

[2] W. E. Gladstone, *Juventus Mundi. The Gods and Men of the Heroic Age* (1869) p. 534: see Jevons, *Money and the Mechanism of Exchange,* pp. 16, 21.

Homeric poems you have the purposes of money clearly separated. Gold was the store of value; it was also used often as the measure of value. Prices are sometimes named or referred to in terms of gold, but the medium of exchange was oxen wh. were also sometimes used as a measure of value.

I don't gó into the historical part of money. It shows that almost every commodity is capable of acting as money. Every kind of merchandise has the two essential properties of money: of measuring and representing value and in this sense merchandise is money and reciprocally all money is essentially merchandise.*

Keep these propositions in mind in order to keep free of fallacies.

By long habit we have come to associate with money the peculiar characteristics of money and so we cannot separate the purposes of money. But a historical view of the subject shows, to begin with, that almost any material can be used as money. It amounts to this: that the earliest money consisted in skins of animals, that when nations became civilised the animals themselves became currency, but when still more civilised and settled down, then corn and other products, then various articles of manufacture – gems, etc.

In the progress of time it has become more and more evident that certain metals have properties peculiarly valuable for money. But to see the truth of the proposition which Turgot laid down:— "gold and silver are constituted by the nature of things money, and universal money, independently of all financial law."[3] Now, this is a very important statement, but to see its truth – we must analyse the qualities wh. money must possess. They have been stated with some fullness, but first of all the question arises must the *material* of money possess utility? Would it be possible for a government to create a money out of any metal they like to use for the purpose? As a matter of fact, probably, no govt. has ever been able arbitrarily to constitute money independently of the utility of the material, and Chevalier and others hold that utility, i.e. intrinsic value of the material – as they wd. call it – is the first essential of a circulating medium.[4] It is requisite in order that you should get people to accept the money, and this is confirmed by the fact that all bank notes have bn. introduced as representative of metallic or other useful money. Money not possessing what is usually called intrinsic value is a kind of makeshift, or in substitution of something else. The question arises whether such a

---

* French Financier. (H. R.)

[3] The exact words which appear in the English translation of Turgot's *Reflexions* are: 'Gold and silver are constituted, by the nature of things, money, and universal money, independent of all convention, and of all laws' – *Reflections on the Formation and Distribution of Riches*, § 43 (London, 1793) p. 28. The passage noted by Rylett as from a 'French Financier' is in fact a quotation from Turgot's *Reflections*, §§ 39 and 40.

[4] Chevalier, *Cours d'Economie Politique*, III, 1. The 'others' referred to by Jevons evidently included Dupre de Saint-Maur, whose *Essai sur les monnaies*, p. 9 is quoted by Chevalier, loc. cit., p. 4.

thing as cowery [*sic*] shells* may be used as money. First, they were used as ornaments.[5]

One all important point is the *force of custom*. When once you have got people to use certain money they will continue to use it tho' it be very much altered in appearance or not. You can depreciate the money, reduce the nature of it and so on, provided that you don't go so far as to break through their custom altogether.

Portability – a certain proportion between the bulk and value of the article. This is obvious.

Indestructability is more or less desirable – tho' not absolutely essential.

Homogeneity, i.e. similarity of quality – which is requisite to make the value equal to each other.

Divisibility is requisite in order that we may divide up values – but not divisibility of a physical nature – but divisibility without destroying the value of that which is divided. The peculiarity of gold, and some other metals, is that you can divide them and melt them together again, so that each part bears equal proportion to each other.

Stability of value – that refers to the use of money as a standard of value and by some authors it has been placed as a very high quality of money. Some put it first. But the question is whether it can be said to be a requisite when it hardly exists in gold or silver. There is very little doubt that in the last 100 years the value of gold and silver has varied 100 per cent and several times over to the extent of 5 or 50 per cent. I apprehend that people generally have no idea of the medium by which they estimate values. But stability of value is an ambiguous term because it depends upon the length of time over which you count. Some things are stable for a year and not after. Now gold and silver money are distinguished as being steady in value for short periods. That arises from this simple fact, that they are indestructible, so that additions or subtractions from the supply operate upon a whole stock not upon annual additions. e.g. Suppose the produce of the world is 50 millions a year, then suppose there was a sudden demand for 50 millions of gold, it would absorb the whole supply, and you wd. think it wd. raise the value of gold. But it does not operate only upon the annual supply. In short gold and silver are things in which the annual supply or consumption does not probably exceed more than two or three per cent at the most. But though permanent in value for short periods they are far from being permanent over long periods – for two reasons. First of all there is the question of purchases. People may make engagements to sell things for gold and silver and create a prospective supply of silver for any amount.[6] That is the cause of

[5] Cf. Jevons, *Money and the Mechanism of Exchange*, pp. 24–5, 33.

[6] It seems probable that Rylett here telescoped two separate sentences in which Jevons was

many of the variations of value which take place. Another cause of the variation is the way in which it is replaced by paper money, that is to say that the whole gold or silver money of the people may be poured suddenly out – as was the case with France, Italy, and so on. Then sudden supplies of metal thrown upon the market must affect the whole. The Bank of France has accumulated the immense stock of 70 millions sterling of bullion, that then must have the effect of depressing the supply and increasing the value of bullion.[7]

In the early part of the century, the first 15 years, almost the whole of the European countries, including England, replaced their metalling; then there must have been an enormous supply compared with the demand.

Gold and silver then are not stable in value when we look over periods of ten or 20 or even less years. Smith held that labour was the ultimate and most stable measure of value,[8] but that breaks down from the impossibility of finding what you mean by labour and that different labourers are competing at such immensely difft. rates. But another suggestion is more practical, namely that corn is one of the most stable things we have. Corn has this peculiarity. It is very variable for short periods on account of the weather. But it is improbable that there is ever any very long succession of bad harvests really. Then over long periods corn is necessarily stable because the principal substance and therefore it is the natural measure of utility.

The last is cognisability, which is a somewhat new term merely designed to express the fact that you can distinguish it from other substances, and gold and silver are most remarkable in this respect.

Chap. VIII of "Money".[9] You cannot define £1 sterling, but might do it in this way: a £1 sterling consists of gold coin, coined and issued by the mint in accordance with the provisions of the coinage act,

---

endeavouring to explain the effect on the value of the precious metals of movements into and out of hoards.

[7] The convertibility of the French franc had been a casualty of the Franco-Prussian War. Cash payment was suspended in 1870 and not resumed until 1 January 1878; but as soon as the indemnity to Prussia was paid, in 1873, the gold reserve of the Bank of France grew quickly. According to figures published about this time it had risen by £12 million between 1865 and 1875 and stood at £64.4 million on 31 December 1875. Contemporary authorities such as Bagehot saw this influx of bullion into France as placing the Bank of England, which was maintaining convertibility with smaller reserves, in a potentially vulnerable position. See Sir John Clapham, *The Bank of England: a history 1694–1914* (Cambridge, 1944) II, 186–7; W. Bagehot, *Lombard Street* (1873; twelfth edition, 1908) pp. 337–9; *Bankers' Magazine*, 36 (1876) 282.

[8] 'Labour alone, therefore, never varying in its own value, is alone the ultimate and real standard by which the value of all commodities can at all times and places be estimated and compared' – *Wealth of Nations*, book I, chapter v; I, 35.

[9] Jevons, *Money and the Mechanism of Exchange*, pp. 67–85.

which has not been subsequently defaced and weighs at least 122½ grains. The difficulty which arises is that coins in use get worn. So that the legal current weight does not necessarily coincide with the legal weight. I am not quite plain myself as to whether you have any right to demand that the coin shall be standard weight = 123.274 grains. And if you receive any new coin it will be pretty nearly of that weight, including the alloy (pure is 113.00160). Page 70 and few following pages where a distinction is described which is practically recognised frequently between money and account and difference of value. The unit of value is that wh. is made a point of reference but it might be made into 100 coins. Note Gresham's law page 80 which is to the effect that if there be money of difft. metallic value in circulation some lighter than others, there is a tendency for the lighter kinds to remain in circulation and for the heavier kinds to be withdrawn.[10]

We proceed with the subject of metallic money – on account of an event wh. is happening at present, namely depreciation of silver exceeding what has ever been known before. Great difficulties arise from the fact that you cannot do with one single metal as a currency and yet it is difficult to employ more than one. The reason that you cannot do with one is that it will be either too valuable for the small coins or too little for the greater ones. How the Anglo Saxons did with only silver I don't know. Most peoples have two metals and we actually employ three. The mode of combining these three varies, but I won't go into the details much because they will be found in the book on "Money" Chap. XI.[11] The capital employed is in currency by weight = meaning that equal weights of each kind of metal may be struck into coins and then they may be allowed to circulate according to the market rates without any attempt to regulate how many pieces of gold shall be made of either. In short allowing these little pieces of metal to be bought and sold like any other commodity. It is true that even these may be divided. The simple currency by weight may take place without the metal being made into coin at all. It may be done by scales as in the early time. That is provided by the name of the coin, and you have the metal coined in pieces which being of equal weight may circulate by probably the number corresponding to the weight. That has never been done as a distinct act of government, though it was proposed in the French Revolution.[12] It was proposed to have ten pieces of gold and silver, and then these were to be

[10] For details of Jevons's investigations into the condition of the gold coinage in 1868 and his role in the ensuing controversy, see Vol. III, Letters 315–21 and notes thereto, pp. 206–21.

[11] Jevons, op. cit., pp. 122–34.

[12] Ibid., pp. 92–3.

sold at market rates. But if you wanted to change the gold pieces you would have to consider what was the value of money in last week's *Economist*, say. It might be $15\frac{5}{8}$ – but if you wanted three coins of silver the difference wd. be $12\frac{5}{8}$. But supposing you wanted to pay $39\frac{1}{4}$ silver pieces for a gold piece you would have many complications. This mere counting of pieces is the inconvenience of producing arithmetical sums and that is a sufficient objection to it.

Then I may say, the principal distinction between the remaining systems is this. They are what has been called monometallic or bi-metallic. These names have been proposed since I finished this book, and I don't mean to say they are perfect ones. A mono-metallic money is that in which the principal metal forms a single legal tender, i.e. where all sums of money are ultimately expressible as amounts of one metal. For instance every expression in our money really means so much gold. You may say that 13/4 means 13 pieces of silver, 4 pieces of bronze, but that is only in a kind of technical point of view. In a commercial point of view it really means $\frac{2}{3}$ of a pound of gold, because 13/4 are only counters or representative pieces standing for a subdivision of a sovereign and of course if you have many 13/4's to receive then they resolve it into gold and you are paid in a single mass of gold. The bi-metallic money, on the contrary, is that in wh. either of two metals is a legal tender – tho' the expression legal tender is one of some difficulty. It may be taken to mean this, that it is that in which debts are legally expressible and payable. It seems to resolve itself into a truism. If you contract a debt in English sterling money it may be paid in English gold sovereigns, but I cannot find out that there is any necessity that you should contract your debts in English gold coin. There is no reason why you should not trade in anything you like, if you can get people to bargain with you. But it is customary to bargain in the money of the country. Then the government provided by the coinage act the kind of coin in general use.

Coming to bi-metallic money it used to be expressed by double standard or double legal tender. That means that a debt may be acquitted in either of two metals. This system had existed even in England in previous centuries. It was adopted by the French Revolution. The point is this, a debt in France could be paid either in gold or silver. Francs of silver contain five drachms.

5 grains std. silver $\dfrac{9}{10}$ = 4·5 grains pure silver = 1 franc

100 ,, ,, ,, ,, = 90 ,, ,, ,, = 20 ,,

Weight of the 20 franc piece of gold 6·457. To get pure gold subtract $\dfrac{1}{10}$ part wh. wd. be 5·806.

It follows that if the market price does not exactly correspond with $15\frac{1}{2}$

ratio it must be more profitable to pay in the one than in the other.

Subsequently to this law the value of silver fell a little below 15½ and remained there all the time up to 1849. Then everybody in France who had a debt to pay might pay in either and they did it in silver [and the whole currency was silver. Discovery of gold in California and Australia led to rise in silver][13] because gold was less valuable – because there was a profit of 1½ per cent on transactions in gold. And it came into use and between 1849 and 1860 about 100 millions of gold coin had been coined and the whole currency became gold. That is double standard.

English writers have condemned this system because it is not a double standard. It is an ordinary standard. If gold falls it becomes the standard and so with silver. The system has been adopted in France, Spain, Belgium for a time, and perhaps Switzerland. English writers objected to this.

In 1860 (?) however the price of silver began to fall again because perhaps production began to increase by Americans discovering silver in the Rocky Mountains and partly because the gold supplies did not keep up to the original point.

Silver got below $5^s\ 0\frac{13^d}{16}$ and the French would have replaced gold money by silver money. Pleasant prospect! because you don't like to carry a great weight in your pocket and government suspended the coinage of silver and came to an agreement with adjoining nations that a certain amount of francs might be struck every year – but this entirely abrogated the effect of the double standard because it prevented the silver coin taking the place of the gold coin.

But now the question is – on one hand Germany determined to reform the whole coinage of the empire. The Germans had in previous years practically silver coinage, but they have determined upon a gold coinage – but have not carried it out yet but the effect will be to absorb a large sum of gold and force upon the market a large sum of silver. Just at this time the Americans have been successful in their silver mines and the consequence is the great fall in the price of silver until it has got down to something like 52^d instead of 60. The fall is unprecedented.

Until the last century or two the ratio of gold to silver was about 10 to 1.

	Herodotus	13 – 1
Plato &	Homer	12 – 1
	Menander	10 – 1
	Livy 189 bc	10 – 1 δεκα ταλαντον

The Æolians having got into some difficulty had to pay a tribute and they were allowed to give ten talents – of silver – or one talent of gold if they liked.

---

[13] Rylett inserted this passage in the margin of the original manuscript.

The rate of the value of gold appeared to fall. It is rather doubtful, but it is said by Suetonius in his life of Caesar that Julius C. got so much plunder out of the cities and temples that gold became quite a drug and the ratio was altered to 9 to 1 – the lowest value for gold in old times.

It seems to have remained very much the same except that it gradually returned to the old rates and in the 14th and 15th centuries it was 12 to 1 or between that and 10 to 1.

As a rule silver seems to have fallen in value more rapidly than gold since Middle times.

In Holland in 1589 it was $11\frac{3}{5}$ to 1
In Flanders   1641 $12\frac{1}{2}$ to 1
In France $13\frac{1}{2}$ to 1
    Spain   14   to 1
(Might take $13\frac{1}{2}$ as mid of 17th centy.)
In Amsterdam   1751 $14\frac{1}{2}$ to 1 [14]

We are now getting up to between 16 and 17 to 1. There is a panic about silver, because people don't know how much it is going to fall. The fall amounts to something like 10 per cent, and if it should continue to fall during this year a person wd. really lose a considerable sum by holding silver.

Panic = people have not any definite ideas of what is going to happen. We must wait until somebody buys the German silver.

Wolowski [15] wrote a series of books predicting that the application of the double standard would produce this fall in price, but he pointed out that if nations insisted on having a gold currency and turning out silver, that there must be a drop in silver. Mr. Cernuschi [16] is making himself very prominent saying that the only course in the present state of the silver market is to return to the double standard. But the point to consider is, can this be done and is it desirable that it should be done. No doubt Germany might have adopted a double standard with the least trouble and France might have kept to it. Then Germany would have kept its silver money, and if France kept its practice France wd. have suffered. Now the currency of France is very large – say 120 millions. Now this sum of silver absorbed and 120 millions of gold given out are enough to alter the market of gold and silver together – decrease the supply and increase the demand. Therefore the value of silver would probably have remained somewhere about $15\frac{1}{2}$ to 1 and we should have avoided this fall in the

[14] The exact source for these figures has not been established, but they correspond roughly with the less precise figures quoted by Jevons in 'The Silver Question' (1877) – *Investigations*, p. 310.

[15] See Vol. III, Letter 309, p. 196. Wolowski, *L'Or et l'Argent. Question Monétaire. Mémoire lu le 7 octobre 1868 à la Séance des Cinq Académies de l'Institut Imperial de France* (1868: second edition, 1869); *Le Change et la Circulation* (1869); *L'Or et l'Argent* (1870); *Enquête sur la Question Monétaire* (1870).

[16] See Vol. V, Letter 686, p. 139. Cernuschi, *Or et Argent* (1874).

price of silver for a considerable time. But it does not follow that both may not depreciate. Coming to the point what will happen if America goes on producing enormous quantities of silver. Simply that silver will be depreciated considerably but that English* monometallic money it will not affect. The standard of value, gold, will not become more valuable compared with other commodities and it will be only the countries in the east where there is a large silver currency and Germany which will use it, but if we were to introduce a double standard the only result wd. be to continue the depreciation of money which has been going on for some time, and there is no reason why money should be depreciated. We shd. not be justified in making a change wh. wd. threaten a further depreciation of the standard of value. Hundreds of holders of silver coin help this. They have had their silver standard and must abide by the unfortunate circumstances of the discovery of the silver mines; but the English are not bound suddenly to make a change wh. would rob fixed incomes in England, in order to have fixed incomes in India. I don't believe the price of silver really will fall. The German government threaten to sell 40 millions of silver all at once just when the American mines are producing much silver, but if people once get the idea that silver is going to rise it will rise and in that way the check will keep it from falling.

(Read the chapters on the subject)[17]

(Credit follows).

LECTURE XVIII

CREDIT

This is a portion of the subject of the utmost importance. Credit, broadly regarded, comprehends all cases where property is made over temporarily to the use of another person. In the case of the Esquimaux, if a family has two boats and another has none he is expected to lend one of his and if lost there is no more heard of it. In a more doubtful system it is the common thing for any one having superfluous capital to put it to the use of those who want capital and the general word credit may be said to cover the whole of such transfers tho' it is generally restricted in

* ? (H. R.)
[17] Jevons, op. cit., chapters XI, XII and XIV, pp. 123–49, 166–88.

commercial language to briefer transfers. You don't generally consider if a man lends money to a railway on perpetual bond that he gives credit to the railway, but it is only one extreme form of the same sort of credit. But the word is ambiguous. Credit often means that esteem, that good opinion of a man which leads other people to give him credit, i.e. to trust him to keep his promise. In this way credit may be a most valuable thing to a man. It does not create capital, but it may evidently enable a man to obtain capital. So that it is as good as creating it, and some men who manage to inspire confidence in their skill and trustworthiness can thereby make extraordinary fortunes. Rothschilds must have made their fortunes in that way. Nathan had £80 and went to London with something less than a million. [1] Again credit means the actual amount of money involved in a particular loan. To give credit is to lend a sum of money for a certain time under certain conditions. Of course there are two sides of the question. Locke defines credit as the expectation of money to come in some limited time. [2] But that of course is on the side of the creditor and has a correlative *expectation** of money having to go on the side of the debtor. But then different acts of giving credit vary in a great many difft. circumstances. Then we may have to discriminate first of all the sum of money or the amount of value for which credit is given, secondly the probable interval of time elapsing before its return, thirdly the probability that it will be paid, and then 4thly there is the rate of interest likely to prevail in the meantime, and fifthly may be mentioned the particular legal form in which the deed is embodied which gives rise to various little personal difficulties. Now these credits may be described in various terms. One of the commonest kinds of credit is "book credit", where the creditor merely enters an account of what is due to him in his own books, as in an ordinary shop purchase on credit. Thus of course there is no evidence of the debt on the part of the debtor, but legally a tradesman's books are receivable as evidence so far as they go, that is, the fact of an entry being made is a presumption that something is due, tho' of course it don't prove it. You will find details in the book on *Money*. [3] Legally speaking the minutiae are very perplexing.

But what we have to look to chiefly is the length of time the credit runs. This may vary from a few hours up to perpetuity. The amount of credit in the case of an ordinary bank cheque is very little indeed, because at any rate it is very little if you are in a town where the cheque is payable

---

[1] Nathan Meyer Rothschild (1777–1836), third of the five sons of the founder of the firm, Meyer Armschel Rothschild (1743–1812), went to London from Frankfort in 1798 to establish the first branch of the House of Rothschild with a capital of about £20,000. He later became head of the London Bank. See Count Corti, *The Rise of the House of Rothschild* . . . (1928) pp. 40–1.

[2] Locke, *Further Considerations concerning raising the Value of Money, Works* (1823 ed) v, 148.

* ?   (H. R.)

[3] Jevons, *Money and the Mechanism of Exchange*, chapters XIX and XX, pp. 238–62.

because at the worst you can go straight to the bank and present the cheque for payment and in a few hours you know whether the debt will or will not be paid. Then it is quite the usual custom for all bank cheques to be presented the next day.

Now it is customary among Political Economists to talk of bank cheques as important forms of credit. We quite agree that they are impt. forms of credit; but then they are forms as it were of very little credit, because the credit only runs over say 24 hours. Therefore the amount of outstanding cheques existing at any one moment can never be very considerable, and cheques are exactly the same as what may be called due bills, i.e. a bill which is due to be paid at any moment: and bank notes are only another form of due bills. But then other commercial bills are distinguished in their very essence from these – not to be paid for 3 months after date, for instance. These involve credit very considerably because three months is something like 90 days and therefore a bill for £100 due three months hence involves 90 times as much credit as a cheque for the same sum – the credit involving the length of time as well as the sum of money.

Bills of exchange are usually limited to something like 12 months at the very most – generally three months. That is owing to the fact that these bills refer to circulating capital. They are what are employed in the manufacture and distribution of circulating capital, wh. therefore only remains for a few months at most in the hands of any one person. Their function is to enable any merchant or manufacturer to provide a circulating capital beyond his own narrow means, and being all withdrawn at short usance there can be no great harm done, i.e. any lender of money will only have a few months to trust the merchant and if he sees that his business is becoming great then he can keep clear of him for the future.*Altho', unfortunately, that prudent course is not always followed, yet it is the foundation of the short runs of most mercantile bills. Then if a man wants fixed capital, he ought not to attempt to raise it by short dated paper. In fact it is a fundamental principle of commerce that the credit shall be proportioned to the fixity of the capital in which it is concerned. Thus a man has absolutely no right to borrow money at short date, and then go and invest it in building. But tthis rule is perpetually broken. A few years ago it was broken habitually by railway companies, who borrowed money before the construction of railway lines upon 3 and 5 years debentures. Now a debenture differs a little from a bill in the fact that interest is payable half yearly; but in other respects it does not differ. But the same thing is existing now in the case of many other undertakings, in building societies, for example.

* ? (H. R.)

So the existence of credit is almost co-extensive with any kind of industry.

Now, the tendency is more and more for the owners of capital to put it into the hands of those who can make most efficient use of it = thus we have people lending money to corporations, or dock bonds, which is perpetual credit. The money is added and nothing more is heard of lent interest.[4] Then, again, the largest example of credit of all is the national debt wh. is interminable except at the will of the government in paying it off.

Now various fallacies have arisen out of the use of credit, and one now supported is that credit is capital. That is false taken absolutely. Instead, credit is the transfer of capital. It never ceases, but only makes much more efficient, i.e. it puts it into the hands of those who make the best use of it. But the question might arise is credit always beneficial? and I apprehend that the answer is that it is almost always beneficial, with certain exceptional cases. Some of these cases will be the kind of fraudulent credit representing what are known as accommodation bills, i.e., those drawn where the employment of the loan does not really correspond to what it pretends to be. But the case of the [Messrs?] Collie sufficiently explains what accommodation bills are.[5]

Another hurtful form, i.e., where credit is given to the consumer, i.e., where the person purchases and consumes and then pays for it afterwards. Except in peculiar cases that is against all doctrines of political economy because sometimes it is not paid for. The objection to it is that it really is drawing capital from profitable investments in trade and putting it into improfitable expenditure. In fact, it is not investment of capital at all. It is rather the opposite – it is contrary investment. Capital assists industry, facilitates industry, and the capital of the manufacturer of woollen goods, for instance, assists the cheap production of woollen goods. But, then, if the tailors capital is invested for 12 or 18 months it does not facilitate industry. It leads to an expenditure very often unwarranted and not met by those who expend and which in no way facilitates production or distribution at all. Therefore credit in this form is a drain on the capital of the country.

Worst form of all is the case of poor people buying on credit.

How far credit can take the place of currency. It has been represented

---

[4] Rylett wrote 'lent interest' and did not subsequently query or correct this, but it seems probable that this was a slip of the pen and that what he intended to write was 'loan interest'. The point which Jevons was endeavouring to make seems to have been that public utilities enjoyed a credit standing which enabled them to issue long-term bonds, rather than having to borrow repeatedly over short periods.

[5] Alexander Collie & Co., a firm of East India merchants, failed in July 1875 with substantial liabilities. See Vol. IV, Letter 496, n. 2, p. 210.

that a bill is itself as good as money. Prof. Walsh, of Dublin,[6] has pointed out pretty clearly that if there is a three months bill drawn, say by A upon B, and then accepted by B, it really amounts to a promise of B to pay this bill when due three months hence. That bill may be endorsed by A to C, and from C to D and so on and bills actually occur in commerce with their backs covered with endorsements from one to another. And, then, it is an actual legal practice. Then it is said every such endorsement constitutes a payment of money, and the bill so far serves as credit. And no doubt that is true so far as it is done. There may be an economy of money, but then it should be added that every bill involves a payment of money: before the bill is discharged there must be a payment of money in some form or other. Of course in the case of bank notes, which are due bills the economy of money is transparent and obvious and it is distinguished by this fact that no legal difficulties or liabilities can arise. The legal meaning of currency of a bank note is that what is called the holder for value is a legal holder and his position is not invalidated by the previous history of the note. That is, supposing I have a £5 bank note in my pocket and it turned out that that note had been stolen by somebody: then the question arises, does the person from whom it was stolen have a claim upon my £5 note? No, and that is the distinction between that and other property. A ring, for instance, could be reclaimed. We find that currency continually discharges debt, and releases people from liabilities and the question really cannot be opened is currency your property or not, except in the case of distinct charge of fraud.

Then again as to the replacement of currency by credit, the question is almost set on a shelf for this reason, that such an enormous part of the payments of the country are now performed by cheques, the clearing of cheques and whether bills of any length of usance economise currency or not is a minor question. The economy of currency is in the use of cheques.

Read account of Clearing House and Banking system in Book on Money.[7]

Pass to Foreign exchanges.

[6] Richard Hussey Walsh, 'Observations on the Gold Crisis, the Price of Silver and the Demand for it; with answer to the question, What becomes of the New Supplies of Gold', *Journal of the Dublin Statistical Society*, I (1855–6) 186–7.
[7] Jevons, op. cit., chapters xxi and xxii, pp. 263–98.

LECTURE XIX

FOREIGN EXCHANGES

Part of the subject consists in considering the way in which the exchanges are adjusted or effected by means of paper documents. I have briefly pointed out in the Chapter on Foreign Bills of Exchange how in early times trade necessarily took the form of Barter.[1] The caravan carried goods on way and exchanged them for other goods, or it was the custom for the ship to take out a cargo and sell it and bring back another. And money need not be carried. But that is barter: but in going to trade by money you come to this that every cargo sent would have to be paid for by money. Therefore the device of bills of exchange has been hit upon, which is simply a mode of making the exports pay for the imports and reducing the trade back again to the form of barter. In the case of a bill of exchange we have to distinguish the drawer, i.e. the person who draws the order, from the drawee. The latter has the bill presented sooner or later. Then by accepting or disowning it he allows that he has the debt to pay or not. Then the ways in which these bills are usually [drawn:]

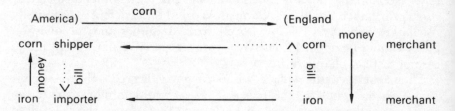

This is the way trade might be done, and is done in many cases, and would be done but for the fact that the Americans get credit from the English.

The bill could be sold to the corn merchant who if he paid money for the bill*

The result is that one clearing in our clearing house and one in America have enabled corn to be cleared off against iron. That rests upon the supposition that the amount of corn is exactly equal to the amount of iron which wd. be an artificial supposition. But what can't be done with one trade might be done with another. If the whole of the goods exported in one direction equalled those in another direction it wd. be possible by drawing these bills of exchange to balance off the whole of the imports agst. the exports and vice versa. So the use of these foreign bills of

---

[1] Jevons, *Money and the Mechanism of Exchange*, chapter XXIII, pp. 299–308.
* ?   (H. R.)

exchange is then to convert international trade into barter again. The principal part of the bills are seldom payable at sight, usually from 3 to 6 months after date. The trade is effected in such a way that it is usually the English merchants who allow the payments of the American merchants to be deferred, that is to say that the English give credit to foreign purchasers and don't take so much credit in their own purchases. This way of drawing bills is not the usual way. It is usually done by a more complex process of drawing on London. This is the way trade is reduced to – to the $\frac{\text{application}}{\text{obligation}}$ of credit involved.*

But let us consider what will happen if the goods in one direction don't equal those moving in another. Supposing that the English iron will not pay for the American corn as sometimes happens. In that case the bills upon America will not be sufficient to pay. Then what will take place? As the English corn merchant has not sufficient bills to send to America, what must he do? He must send money, and that costs money. The cost to the United States is not much less than 1%. Say that the cost of transmitting specie is 1%, it follows that if that merchant could go and buy bills at $\frac{3}{4}$ per cent premium he would save $\frac{1}{4}$ per cent. The actual piece of paper enabling him to acquit his debt will be worth at least $\frac{3}{4}$ per cent. He will save by sending a bill. The matter assumes some complexity if we take into account the difference of money. Supposing all countries had an international money and used sovereigns, then when the English exports will not pay for the imports from America there will be a premium upon bills upon America.

> Exports too little
> Imports too great
>
> ———————————
>
> Premium on foreign bills
> Rate of exchange falling
> Additional profit to exporters
> And loss to importers

How is this to be expressed in money? How much money in America you can buy by a certain amount of money in England. If the corn merchant has £100 in his own safe, how much can he purchase down in America under the present state of things? The rate . . . .* [2] Now

* ? (H. R.)
* ? (H. R.)
[2] Assuming that Jevons was following out the example he had previously given, the phrase which Rylett did not catch here would presumably have been some such words as 'The rate will be below par'.

what will it be in America? or what will be the effect upon trade in England. There is naturally a tendency in the foreign exchanges to adjust themselves, so that exports shall exactly equal imports. What are the causes of the variations of price of the foreign bill? These are very numerous, but may be divided into 1. Nominal variation of the exchanges due to depreciatn. of the coinage or it may be to the paper currency. Par of exchange = that quantity of the coin of the country which contains a quantity of metal exactly equal to a unit of coin of the other country.

Francs 25.22 = £1

25.22 francs gold = £1

The quality the same – pure gold.

This is complicated by different coinages in silver and gold. Another difficulty is that some countries charge a mint charge for coining money. The French make a mint charge.[3] Supposing it costs, say, $\frac{1}{3}$ p.c. to coin money in one country more than another that affects the par of exchange because before you can get the coin in the other country you must send the metal and get it coined and pay this $\frac{1}{3}$ per cent. Therefore the par of exchange does not exactly coincide with our definition. It always was thought to do so. But you should add this: the par of exchange will be defined allowance being made for the differences of mint charge.* But if the coinage of a country is very bad, got worn a good deal, then the rate of exchange would rise of course. But of course this wd. be a new par of exchange.

This occurs, again, in the depreciation of paper money because all governments assume that the paper money issued is the money of the place. Then suppose this money is depreciated the same effect wd. take place, as if the coins were depreciated. The Italians' paper money was depreciated 15 per cent.[4] Then the course of exchange would be with the depreciated 15 per cent, the rate of exchange would be 29 lire for £1 sterling.

But now we come to the real fluctuation – which arises from the inequality of trade for instance. But here we must discriminate between

---

[3] For Jevons's comments on mint charges in his 1868 paper 'On the Condition of the Metallic Currency of the United Kingdom', see *Investigations*, pp. 250–5. Cf. above, p. 99.

* ?   (H. R.)

[4] 'The chief financial result of the 1866 war was the large scale resort to credit. Scialoia had to issue 650 million lire worth of paper money and eompel acceptance of nonconvertible notes of the Banca Nazionale. . . . As an immediate result, money lost much of its value, and the "forced currency" further lowered national credit. The bank gained handsomely, but coin left for France at an alarming rate, and the inflationary effect of a fall in money values reduced the real wages of the people. . . .' – Denis Mack Smith, *Italy: a Modern History* (Ann Arbor, 1959) p. 87. For details of the effects of the Italian suspension of cash payments between 1866 and 1883, introduced by Antonio Scialoia (cf. Vol. IV, Letter 565, n. 3, p. 303), see James Bonar's review of Camillo Supino, *Storia della Circolazione Bancaria in Italia, 1860–94* (Turin, 1895) in the *Economic Journal*, 5 (1895) 600–2; also Banca d'Italia, *I bilanci degli istituti di emissione italiani 1845–1936*, 2 vols (Rome, 1967) I, lxix.

the fluctuation which arises from the balance of trade and that which arises from the rate of interest, because if the bill has long to run, and the rate of interest is high, that causes the value of the bill to fall. A larger discount has to be subtracted. But this is avoided if we take short bills or short exchange i.e. where a bill is payable at sight or within a few days after sight. In that case the buyer of the bill is out of pocket only during the time of the transmission of the bill and the few days remaining for presentation. Of course anywhere between England and most parts of the Continent the bill reaches in two days and if it is a bill at sight it is paid the very day it arrives and then interest does not intervene. Thus of course it is short exchange wh. exhibits the real variation of exchanges.

The curious point is this – there are some countries that will have the exchanges against them. Countries producing gold and silver will have the exchanges always agst. them. The cost of export is, say, 1 per cent. Then exchange would be 1 per ct. agst. that country. Australia. e.g. The wool goes away at one time, and what is the effect of the sudden export of Australian wool? It makes the exchange more in favour of Australia.

Read Goschen on "Theory of Foreign Exchanges".[5]

Take Mr. Goschen as our guide on the subject of Foreign Exchanges.

It is important to comprehend exactly the influences upon Foreign Exchanges and the difficulty is this, that it is a question both of amount and time. The general principle we came to the other day was that the whole of the exports must balance the whole of the imports – but the question is – within what time must that balance take place? If England has to pay France a certain sum now and France will have to pay England six months hence can those two amounts be made to balance?

Now if there were people with money to share who could discount the debt that may be made to balance the debt,* but Mr. Goschen gives an interesting analysis of all indebtedness and the way in which they arise.[6] First we must put down imports, actual goods to be paid for. Second – purchase of shares, of public securities. Third payments of porters, commissions, tribute, etc. Fourth, expenses of foreign residence and travel. Fifth, payment of freights. All these equally affect the exchanges because they give rise to money debts and in fact are ordinary money debts. Even public securities may be regarded as a debt, and these things passing from one country to another represent a great deal of our commerce. A man may take over to America the value of a million sterling but nobody knows it is going except the few individuals

[5] George Joachim, Viscount Goschen (1831 – 1907), *The Theory of Foreign Exchanges* (1861). See Vol. V, Letter 633, n. 1, p. 85.

* ? (H. R.)

[6] Goschen, op. cit., chapter II, 'Analysis of International Indebtedness considered as the basis of the Foreign Exchanges', seventh edition (1866) pp. 11–22.

concerned. That mystifies the balance of trade as it is called. Again foreign residence produces debt. If a wealthy Englishman goes and lives in Italy he expends his substance there and a certain sum of money is owing from his agents in England to him. In what form is it to be sent?

It is at this point perhaps that we may enter upon the explanation of the immense difference that may exist between the exports and the imports as given in the custom house accounts. The imports appear to exceed the exports, so that it would seem as if we were always losing by trade.

In former days the mercantile theory was to the effect that the whole benefit of trade consisted in the difference between these exports and imports. So that when the imports exceed the exports it wd. seem as if there were some loss. But I dare say you have read sufficient about the mercantile theory. It arose simply from confusion between the idea of money and wealth – confusion arising out of the fact that wealth is held in the form of money – therefore it seemed that the increase of money in the country must mean the increase of the wealth of the country. Now we perceive clearly enough that the permanent increase of the metallic medium of the country is really of no consequence to the country because the utility of that medium to the country is simply the performance of exchanges. It doesn't matter to you whether you have £10 or £20 in your own purse, provided that you can pay your ordinary expenses equally well as with the other.

In the present day the opposite view is taken – that the benefit of trade consists in importing as much as you can. It is the imports that are our gain because upon them we live.

The difference between the exports and imports accordingly depends upon this: whether England is lending to other countries in a large degree or not. Suppose that in former days the English were going to contract a great loan in favour of the Turks. Then the payment of the money to make that loan involves a disturbance of the exchanges. Since you have agreed to lend a man abroad – then that is a debt from you to that man, and accdgly. when loans are being made abroad then the exchanges will be against this country. So we shall import less and export more.

Then, as Mr. Cairns explains, the loan involves payments of interest. [7] Now, in past years large amounts of money have been lent by the English to many countries and the interest of these accumulates. Hence there is a large amt. of debt from abroad to England which tend to increase the imports from abroad to England. And Mr. Cairns ingeniously shows that if a country went on lending for a long period of time – that would necessarily be the result. Supposing we had bn. lending 10 million a year

[7] See Vol. III, Letter 178, n. 1, p. 16. J. E. Cairnes, *Some Leading Principles of Political Economy newly Expounded* (1874) chapter III, §§ 6 and 7, pp. 359–66.

for 50 years, i.e., 500 millions. Take that at an average of 6 per cent and you get 30 millions a year of interest, i.e., the incoming tribute from foreign nations to ourselves wd. be 30 millions a year. The outgoing wd. be 10 million. So after fifty years we should have a great balance in our favour.

Another point is the payment of freights. I don't profess to understand this but it appears also to increase. There is the same tendency, because an English ship is Eng. property. Nevertheless it is going about the world and earning money. Then many of the freight are bought abroad – bought on delivery. In other cases the ships make cross cargoes. These ships are continually earning money due in England *called* [*] increase of balance.

Another point is this that the exports and imports are priced by the custom house in an English port. So that the imports are put at their original value plus freights and cost of importation, whereas the exports are simply the price without those charges. It is partly the freight that makes the difference there, you see.

Now today we are in a peculiar position – there ha' been a greater and more rapid fall in the rate of interest than ever . The rate is 2 per cent and the market rate is $1\frac{1}{2}$, say. The rate has never fallen so suddenly; and that is explained by the default of the Turkish Egyptian loans, [8] which means a disinclination to lend to foreign countries and that has deranged the exchanges in our favour, namely, that sums are becoming due from abroad here, and people are not investing correspondingly from here to abroad. The diffce. has to come in the form of specie, and specie is accumulating in the bank of England. Then, one readily sees the absurdity of that going on long, because if the bank doubles its amount of bullion, it is of no good to anybody in England. And the fact is that gold in the bank is only wanted to make foreign payments, and if there are no foreign payments to make the gold is a burden upon the market. The result of this state of things must be that there will be a great speculation in Home enterprise. In a short time, however, it will break out into other forms of transportation. Merchants will export goods in a reckless manner, and give long credits to foreigners. They will increase their exports.

In another part of his book Mr. Goschen explains the adjustment of

* ? with (H. R.)
[8] In October 1875 the Turkish Government announced its intention to pay only half the dividend on the loan raised at the end of the Crimean War and guaranteed by the governments of Britain and France: the funds were to be diverted to its internal debt. The security for the loan was the tribute paid by Egypt to the Turkish Government which hitherto had been paid twice yearly into the Bank of England. The majority of bondholders were British and one result of the public outcry at this apparent act of repudiation was the appointment of a Select Committee of the House of Commons on Loans to Foreign States. See *Annual Register* (1875) pp. [114–17]; *Bankers' Magazine*, 36 (1876) 272.

periodic dates.[9] It is partly what I alluded to in the case of Australia, which as I said exported its wool at one period in the year, when the exchanges were in favour of Australia, tho' they were against the colony at all other times. Now, the same thing occurs in Russia and corn growing countries. These export at the end of harvest but their imports come in the spring, or partly all the year round. Now if the corn is exported at the end of the harvest, what is the effect upon the exchanges? They are unfavourable to us, and then all the rest of the year they will be the reverse. Now supposing that was the simple state of things – then there would be a double current of money i.e. when corn came from Russia we should have to send bullion immediately to pay for it, and then it wd. have to come back to us as we exported things that Russia wanted. Now, as Goschen explains, that is prevented in this way – by means of foreign bills of exchange. The bankers when corn is exported can draw what you may call real bills i.e. a bill drawn against actual . . . .[10] sent, and is an order for the importers to pay money for what they have imported. But when a regular seasonal trade is expected and occurs as a regular thing then banks draw bills in anticipation. They get the London merchants to lend them the money in the form of liberty to draw. The Russian merchant will point out to his London correspondent that in two months he will be able to transmit real bills, but in the meantime wants liberty to draw. Getting that, he can draw and the bill is payment so far as appearance goes. But the bill having been presented and paid the English Banker is out of his money: then he will receive it back by the transmission of real bills drawn upon the corn exports. In this way you get over the difficulty of time; you make one debt balance another, the Eng. banker being the one who finds the funds in the meantime. So that after all the thing comes simply to this – the Eng. say to the Russian "We will let you have what you want without paying now because we know that you will pay with corn in two months time." And, as Mr. Goschen shows, accommodation bills in such circumstances are perfectly justifiable as only anticipating a future real debt.

Then we have the arbitration of exchanges. It refers to the indirect settlement of exchanges or the circular settlement of exchanges, because it is quite apparent that any amount of indebtedness might be cleared off in one payment if it only occurs in a proper series of payments. This is the technical rule. Draw upon the place where the arbitrated price is better for that place than the advised price, and remit to the place where it is worst. The arbitrated price is got by multiplying together the rates of exchange of *two** places.

[9] Goschen, op. cit., p. 38.
[10] 'shipments'; Goschen, *Foreign Exchanges,* loc. cit.
* or *all* ?   (H. R.)

A second rule is this: Where the uncertain price is given draw thro' that place which produces the highest arbitrated price and remit thro' that wh. produces the lowest.

The explanation of this is exceedingly simple. It amounts to this: that A would draw bills upon C as an *acknowledgment*† of debt towards A. Then A wd. remit through B, draw bills upon C and send them to B. B sends them to C who should accept and pay.

But the tendency now is to draw on London.[11]

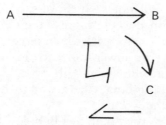

A may draw a bill upon L and forward it to B. Both are good houses. Hence B regards that bill as gold and it may go on circulating and ultimately discharges a debt from C to London, and A must remit other bills to London to balance.

Pass on to Illustrations from Commercial Fluctuations.

LECTURE XX

ILLUSTRATIONS FROM COMMERCIAL FLUCTUATIONS

What is the variation of prices – the course of trade as it varies from year to year? The great question to decide is whether there is such a thing as law in the investment of capital or the undertaking of any new affairs.

It was towards the end of the 17th Century that the commercial history of England began to take its rise. It was then that the banking system sprang up. In 1694 the bank of England was created, and in 1695, the bank of Scotland. It was during this period that one of the intervals of commercial activity took place, e.g. fire insurance companies were started in 1696. Then there followed considerable difficulty. A great many other schemes were started most of which came to nothing. Several great schemes arose. Land, banking, mining, water companies, companies for steam engines, were all started at this period. In the course of three

† or *question?* (H. R.)
[11] Goschen, op. cit., chapter III, 'Examination of the Various Classes of Foreign Bills in which International Indebtedness is ultimately embodied', pp. 23–42.

years most of them collapsed. The money market became in a very bad state, and the government intervened to support merchants of commerce. The Earl of Halifax supported the bank by increasing its capital by four fifths of its sum in Exchequer ties – bonds, and one fifth in bank notes.[1] I know nothing of importance up to the time of the South Sea Bubble, which came to an end in the year 1720. The South Sea Bubble was remarkable taken in connection with the Mississippi Bubble which happened in France a little before. The latter was set afloat by John Law, whose scheme was to issue notes which were to be loaned to land owners in quantities proportioned to the value of their land, so as to produce an enormous currency and then enrich the country. The French adopted the idea and he got into great power under the French government and his scheme was worked in connection with an extraordinary enterprise for employing funds in Louisiana – there was to be a great company to develop that part of the world.[2]

Parallel with this was the South Sea Bubble – so called because it was proposed to establish a great trade with the South Seas of America. They were going to land in various parts of S. America, make settlements, and acquire wealth. It was originally started in 1711. It seems at first to have started in rivalry with the bank of England, and having acquired a financial position, proposed to buy up the public annuities, and ultimately, also, to buy up the bank of England itself. The consequence of this bold proposal was to raise their stock to 126: the prospect that the scheme of purchasing the bank would be carried out made the stock rise to 319. Then a dividend of 10 per cent was voted as the directors were confident they wd. have the business to meet it. And before 2nd June 1720 the stock was 890 per cent, but fell the same evening to 640, yet rose again to 720. They had to make a call, and stock fell; but having got over that the directors were able to call for a new subscription at 1000. This enormous success produced a great group of other bubble companies, almost all imaginable things were projected.* [3]

---

[1] The immediate cause of the first serious crisis to be met by the Bank of England, during a volatile period, was the recoinage of silver money, 1696–9. The failure of the Mint to issue sufficient new money to meet the deadline for the recall of clipped coins led to a run on the Bank in May and June 1696 and partial suspension of cash payments. Charles Montagu (1661–1715), later Earl of Halifax, then Chancellor of the Exchequer, authorised the issue of the first Exchequer Bills in £10 and £5 units, an expedient which relieved the circulation shortage. The Bills were regarded as an alternative to the paper money issued by the Bank, as the survival of that institution was by no means assured at the time. See Clapham, *Bank of England*, I, 34–40.

[2] This was the Compagnie d'Occident, chartered in August 1717. For a recent concise account of its later fortunes, and of the ideas and activities of John Law (1671–1729), see Earl J. Hamilton, 'The Political Economy of France at the Time of John Law', *History of Political Economy*, vol. I, no. 1 (Spring 1969) 123–49.

* See *Popular Illusions.*   (H. R.)

[3] Charles Mackay, *Memoirs of Extraordinary Popular Delusions and the Madness of Crowds*, 2 vols (1841), which included accounts of both the Mississippi Scheme and the South Sea Bubble.

The excitement extended to Poland – so that there was some degree of simultaneity.

But difficulties arose. The South Sea Bubble wanted a monopoly: they went into legal proceedings; a fall in stock began. It fell to 850, and a 30 per cent dividend was declared on 30 Aug. 1720; but as matters got worse they promised to pay 50 per cent for each succeeding year for 12 years. Nevertheless in December the stock was down to 410. People reflected that the Mississippi had collapsed. At the end of 1720 and beginning of 1721, most companies collapsed entirely. The South Sea Company was investigated by Parliament, and existed until lately, because it had bought some annuities.[4]

The lesson is – that there is no limit to human credulity, and that that credulity has the effect (for the time being) of producing value. The shares of these companies were actually sold for gold, and were treated as gold, but as there was no basis of actual industry at the bottom of them they all collapsed. The same thing has happened elsewhere – tulip mania in Holland – fortunes were to be made with tulips – but all fell through.[5]

We pass now to other crises of the same century. In 1763 there seems to have been an era of collapse, following a few years of excitement: and what is very noticeable is that it was simultaneous again with fluctuations in Hamburg and Amsterdam; and it is also noticeable that in these towns at the time there was no such thing as paper currency. Banks existed, but only dealt in bullion, or actual receipts for bullion, and yet this did not prevent a considerable bubble coming out in 1763–4. At the same time there was a considerable amount of bankruptcy in England.

About ten years subsequently a similar collapse occurred, viz, about 1772. The result of extravagant overtrading. A great bank broke in this year, and there was again much bankruptcy, which extended also to Holland and several other parts of Europe.[6]

I would not like to say there was anything of the same sort in 1782. I rather think there was, but it was interfered with by the American war. Prices fell between 1782 and 1786 in the proportion of 100 to 85 – so that there must have been a collapse.

Coming to 1792, we find that this was undoubtedly a year of very great speculation in England and Europe and the United States.

[4] In 1861 Gladstone, then Chancellor of the Exchequer, abolished the £1898 management charge which the Bank of England had taken over from the South Sea Company. See Clapham, *Bank of England*, II, 48, 255–6. See W. R. Scott, *The Constitution and Finance of English, Scottish and Irish Joint-Stock Companies to 1720*, 3 vols (Cambridge, 1910–12) I, 388–438 and III, 288–360, for the full history of the South Sea Company.

[5] A wave of speculation in tulips – the 'tulipomania' – swept Holland from 1634 to 1636. See Mackay, op. cit., second edition (1852) II, 85–92.

[6] The commercial crisis of 1772–3 led to the collapse of a major Scottish bank, Douglas, Heron and Co. of Ayr. The crisis spread from England to the Continent via Amsterdam and its effects were felt as far afield as Sweden and Russia. See Clapham, *Bank of England*, I, 242–9.

Prices varied as follows:—

1782	..	..	..	..	100
1789	..	..	..	..	85
1790	..	..	..	..	87
1791	..	..	..	..	89
1792	..	..	..	..	93
1793	..	..	..	..	99 [7]

But in the autumn of 1792 commercial failures began and in 1793 there was a panic. Three hundred country banks were very much shaken and upwards of one hundred stopped. It was on this occasion that Sir John Sinclair made the attempt to issue Exchequer Bills, and commissioners were now appointed who were to lend to merchants, bankers, and others bills of £100 or £50 each. As soon as the act was passed £70,000 were immediately sent from Manchester to Glasgow. The effect of this paper money was that many who applied for bills did not want them. There were 380 applications to the amount of £3,850,000; but only 280 really received money to the amt. of £2,200,000. When these loans had to be repaid, they were all repaid, and much of it before it was due. Only two firms became bankrupt notwithstanding. After the accounts were closed, however, it appeared that the government had made a profit of £400,000. So by a mere act of Parliament govt. was able to save many firms. [8]

All this is what now occurs at intervals of years. Events, however, were broken up by the exploits of Napoleon and the French Revolution of 1797. On Feb. 25 the Bank of England was stopped by govt. which was in great peril – greater than since the Spanish Armada. There was danger of intervention, and there was a run upon the bank. Everything looked at its blackest. Consols went down to something like 50. In the early part of the year they were down to $47\frac{1}{2}$ – one of the lowest points. On 26th February (the Sunday after Saturday) the govt. prohibited the bank from paying gold, because they thought all the bullion would be gone, and if they went to war there would be a difficulty so that cannot be called a commercial crisis.

Affairs continued in an uncertain state; but in 1807 – 1808, there was a period of commercial fluctuation, but we cannot place any stress on it

---

[7] These index-number figures are taken from Jevons's 1865 paper 'The Variation of Prices, and the Value of the Currency since 1782', reprinted in *Investigations*, p. 144.

[8] The circulation crisis of 1792–3, which caused over one hundred country banks to fail, reached its peak in April and May 1793 with the passing of an Act authorising the issue of £5 million in Exchequer Bills, to be administered by special commissioners. Sir John Sinclair (1754–1835), perhaps best remembered for his *Statistical Account of Scotland*, but who was also M.P. for Caithness and a Director of the Bank, has traditionally been credited with the authorship of this successful scheme. See Clapham, *Bank of England*, I, 260–5; R. Mitchison, *Agricultural Sir John, The Life of Sir John Sinclair of Ulbster* (1962) p. 137.

because it was in a great degree regulated by Napoleon in 1805 and the freeing of the European ports of England.[9]

In 1811–14 there was a further period of want of trade. I cannot make much out of this. There seems at any rate to have been a great fall of prices in 1816.

But passing to the years 1822–1825 we meet the first great bubble of this century. It may be remarked best in the years 1823–4–5. It took its rise in the previous years, no doubt. One of the best marks of this bubble is the number of insurance companies started. In 1820 there was 1; in 1821, 1; in 1822, 1; in 1823, 3; in 1824, 7; 1825, 4; 1826, 1; in 1827 and 1828 none; but in 1829, 1.[10] You may observe it also in the course of prices, tho' the rise was exceedingly short as regards commodities in general. In 1822 general course of prices was 88, 89, 88, 103, showing a very considerable rise. They fell again to 90, 90, 91. But very often the course of speculation is best shown by prices of metals varied in this way:— 100, 107, 108, 123, 111, 103, 95. So there was a complete rise and fall.

Previously, and in the year 1825, there was great speculation abroad. The Spanish Colonies separated from Spain, and there were more companies. Some of them almost comparable to the South Sea Co. The Mexican Company had £10 shares which rose in the end of 1824 to £43 per share, but in January 1825, rose to £120. Another Company, Real de * Mining Co., had £70 shares wh. rose to £1,350 in Jan. 25. and with this foreign speculation the bullion of the bank of England began to go abroad – paid for. And the bullion which had been on the 31st Jan. 1824, 13½ millions, had fallen by Dec. 31st 1825 to 1¼ millions, less than a tenth.[11]

In Nov. 1825 the commercial pressure became very severe, and the great bank at Plymouth was the first to stop. There was running upon other banks. Three or four London banks went and 63 country banks. The bank of England found their bullion so far gone that they wanted the government to prohibit them from continuing payment.

Then a celebrated incident occurred. It was said that the Bank of England was saved by one of its officers who remembered that there was a

[9] The years 1802 and 1806 were peak years in a mild cyclical movement, with troughs in 1804 and 1808. See Gayer, Rostow and Schwartz, *Growth and Fluctuation of the British Economy 1790–1850* (1953) vol. I, chap. II.

[10] On the origins of the rapid expansion of 1822–4 and the part played by promotion of insurance companies in it, see G. Clayton *British Insurance* (1971), pp. 102–5.

* ? (H. R.)

[11] The speculative boom which followed the wars of liberation in the Spanish colonies in South America saw its peak in 1825. Among the mining associations formed to exploit the region's legendary wealth was the Real del Monte Co., to which Jevons evidently referred. See Senior, op. cit., p. 215; D. Joslin, *A Century of Banking in Latin America* (1963) p. 2.

On the financial crisis of 1825 in England, cf. Gayer, Rostow and Schwartz, op. cit., I, chap. IV, especially pp. 202–7.

chest full of £1 notes in the cellar. He suggested that it should be brought up and put on the counter, and it is said that the appearance of this chest allayed the panic. It hardly seems to hold water, however, for one chest of £1 notes would not save anything unless by a mere effect of the imagination.[12]

> *Essay*: How far is there a real increase in value in the case of a bubble company? or How is it that people are found in the case of a Bubble to pay large sums for the scrip or shares. Is the country really richer while they exist than it is after the collapse?

LECTURE XXI

COMMERCIAL FLUCTUATIONS SINCE 1836

The next interval we have to consider is that from 1836–39, i.e. the period of crisis and difficulty. We find that from 1830–40 was a period on the whole of very great prosperity and there was a considerable rise in prices. The variation of metals for instance is shown as follows:—[1]

	Price Index for Metals (Copper, Lead, Tin, Iron) 1782 = 100*	Rate of Discount %	Bills of Exchange created in quarter ending October £ million
1831	80	4	53
2	77	4	47
3	82	$3\frac{1}{2}$	51
4	87	4	55
5	90	4	58
6	114	$5\frac{1}{2}$	78
7	97	$5\frac{1}{2}$	63
8	96	$3\frac{1}{2}$	71
9	94	$6\frac{1}{2}$	82

*Source: Jevons, 'The Variation of Prices, and the Value of the Currency since 1782' (1865) *Investigations*, p. 147

[12] The run on the Bank of England from 11 to 17 December 1825 was halted by the return by the Bank of France of a sufficient quantity of English gold, in return for silver shipped to France. The famous box containing about £400,000 of £1 notes was opened on 16 December and provided a temporary respite. For an account of the banking crisis of 1825, see Clapham, *Bank of England*, 11, 98–102.

[1] In Rylett's manuscript only the three columns of figures were written down; here headings have been supplied for each column in order to clarify the argument.

(30/31/32/33 might be called years of black trade and then it became brisk and came to a maximum in 1836).

With this we may compare the rates of discount. But in connection with the rates of discount it should be remarked they cannot be compared with the variation of rates now, because the usury laws previously existing had the effect of reducing the rates charged, so that they are much more even in appearance than probably they really were. You observe the rate of interest was low in the early part of that time and rose in 1836 to what you may now consider a pretty good rate, and then fell in the interval and rose at the crisis of 1839 a considerable height. This is so good an example of that I may as well give you what no doubt is an all important point – viz. the amount of bills of exchange created. That shows the amount of engagements made (see last column of preceding table).

Now, turning to the events – good harvests occurred from 1830 to 35, until the price of corn fell to the low point of 36/5 (an exceedingly low price – and has hardly occurred since). The effect of the low price of corn is to increase the floating capital of the country. It is the floating capital itself, or the principal item enabling people to live readily and spend freely in other directions. The low prices caused less land to be sold, so that when there came an unfavourable season in 1836, prices rose to 60/-, afterwards in 1838 to 80/-. Now while the price of corn was low – 1833–4–5, there was general prosperity of manufacturers. It was a period when all mechanical manufactures increased rapidly; and then joined to it was a great speculation in foreign loans. Between three and four thousand public companies were started, with a nominal capital of 200,000,000. To show how clearly this gauges the variation of enterprize I give you the insurance companies:—

1831 – 1	This shows just when the Bubble is at its
1832 – 1	highest. When some safe ones have been
1833 – 0	floated, others are prepared to float or sink as
1834 – 2	the case may be.
1835 – 2	
1836 – 6	
1837 – 6	
1838 – 4	
1839 – 1	

This is an instructive interval, because there was a crisis in 1836, and another in 1839. There was a kind of anticipated crisis which did not clear the air. We had a premature crisis in 1872–3 and we may have a stiff one presently. [2]

[2] See Vol. IV, Letters 540, n. 1, and 566, n. 6, pp. 274 and 304; Vol. V, Letter 636A, n. 4, pp. 88–9.

In the autumn of 1836 several banks were on the point of breaking. The bank of England advanced 6 millions suddenly to all who wanted it and thus staved off the difficulty or diminished it. Then the speculation went on again till credit in all commercial parts of the world became very much extended in the autumn of 1839. The bank of Belgium *failed* *in the autumn of 1838. But the worst was in 1839 when there was an enormous break down of American credit. American banks became bankrupt. The effect was communicated to England, and there was a great run upon the bullion of the bank, which went down so rapidly as in July they approached bankruptcy. Their liabilities were nearly 29 millions and their bullion was in . . . . 3 millions, barely more than an 18th part of their liabilities and the drain was continued and it went so far that they would necessarily have been bankrupt. In Aug. it was reduced to 2,400,000 and they would have been bankrupt if they had not got from the bank of France a loan of 2,000,000. They had liberty to draw bills which amounted to exporting so much gold and that was sufficient to save them from actual stoppage.[3]

The effect of this late crisis in 1839 was to reduce trade to a very low state and the following few years were the worst that had ever occurred since the great wars. It was not so bad as 1841 but it was /41,/42,/43 that saw the very lowest state of employment such as we don't know at all in the present day and gave rise to the Chartist disturbances.

But then began the extraordinary mania for railway construction, which suddenly altered the state of things. I can show you the actual numbers as far as we have time.

	Price Index for Metals	Miles
1841	90	1426
2	80	1274
3	71	1161
4	74	1420
5	86	1821
6	90	2040
7	90	2042
8	77	2194
9	73	1461
50	74	1463

There we have the lowest point in 1843 and then a rise. The rise, not so

* ? (H. R.)

[3] For a full account of the circumstances of this French loan, as well as of the whole crisis of 1839 and its causes, see Matthews, *A Study in Trade Cycle History*, especially pp. 89–91 and 172–6.

great as in previous cases, may be due to an improvement in manufactures; but still the demand ran up and then after the crisis of 1847 we see a rapid fall to 73. These are metals generally. The same is true of iron particularly.

Now there is a remarkable series of figures as to the number of *bricks**
made. Again we see the lowest point in 1843, and the largest point comes a year beyond the year 1847, because the works were begun and must be finished. The amount of timber used exactly corroborates this also. Now in the years /44, 45−46 took place the extraordinary railway mania, when everybody who had money put it into railway shares, and the amt. of companies started and the engagements made are extraordinary.

But the main point which brings these speculations to a head is the price of corn. Now in Aug. 1846 a good harvest had brought the price down to 46/-. But then began the failure of the potato crop in Ireland, together with the failure of the corn harvest as well. The effect was such that the price of corn rose in Jan. 1847 to 92/10 which is almost exactly double. Then there was great speculation in the corn trade and attempts to import, but unfortunately for the importers there was a good harvest in 1847 wh. ran down the price and a series of great failures in the corn trade began. But at the same time the entire failure of the potato crop again decreased the food of a large part of the people. However there is no doubt that in 1847 occurred a very sharp crisis when for the first time it became necessary to suspend the bank act passed in the year 1844. Sir R. Peel in advocating this act had expressed his opinion that it would prevent these variations of commerce, but when actually advising the suspension of his own act he confessed that it had not done what he anticipated. But when we see what took place in commerce there was nothing else to expect. These matters are not matters of currency. They involve the whole industry of the country. If we investigated the matter fully we should find a very considerable fraction of the world's population had been during this interval taken away from their ordinary pursuits and devoted to railway making. The number of young men who wanted to become railway engineers was extraordinary. The crisis in 1847 was so sharp and severe that it caused an immediate fall in price and 1848−9 were years of bad trade and considerable distress. Then the Chartists made their last demonstration, which was so unsuccessful that it was the end of their movement.[4]

The discovery of gold in California in 1849 helped the revival wh. came rapidly. Take now the years 1850

* ? (H. R.)
[4] For a contemporary account of these events, see D. Morier Evans, *The Commercial Crisis, 1847−1848* . . ., second edition (1849), reprint (New York, 1969).

	Price Index for Metals	Rate of Discount
1851	73	3.0
2	80	1.9
3	103	3.7
4	109	5.0
5	104	4.6
1856	109	4.9
7	108	6.6
8	96	3.3
9	97	2.8
60	95	4.2

This was not wholly due to commercial causes but rather to the actual gold itself. The rise was very great from /51 to /54. Then '52 and '53 were exceedingly prosperous and great emigration took place. The opening of business with Australia also made trade brisk. The rate of discount is worth notice in these years. The average rate of discount shows a rapid rise to 1854. Then there was a check by the war with Russia in 1854. The effect of war on commerce is to make people uncertain of the future. That is shown in the falls in 1855; and there was a kind of suspense in the progress of work. In the absence of that war no doubt there would have been a great bubble speculation. But we find that even the war didn't prevent the actual progress of the commercial tide. Peace was made in 1856, so that there were just two years of war. Then speculation broke out again. As you see marked by the higher prices of metals in 1856. Then looking to the price of corn we find that in years 1850–1 it was as low as 36/- or 37/- and was low during 1852, concurring with the low rate of discount. We continually find that the periods of excitement are based on prior intervals of low prices of corn. But subsequently to that there was a failure of harvest. 1854 to 1856 were dear years of corn. Prices rise to 96/-. The crisis itself again was caused by American traders. There was in fact an enormous series of failures in Aug. 1857 in the United States, certain credit institutions having broken down. In the end of September 1857 150 banks in America suspended payment. There was an enormous depreciation of all kinds of American property from 10 to 80 per cent. The effect of this was to lead English capitalists to suddenly invest whatever they could spare in American property; and this happened just at the time of year when it is found in England that there is a demand for money, partly by the payment of *dividend** early in Oct. – but no doubt helped by the previous overtrading there was a run upon the bank almost. On the

* ?   (H. R.)

8th of Oct. the bank raised its rate from $5\frac{1}{2}$ to 6 per cent. On the 12th Oct. a special meeting of directors raised it to 7 per cent, that is probably the sharpest rise up to that time. Now, *a big bank* [run] *set in. Property*† was depreciated from 10 to 35 per cent. On the 12th Oct. a large Glasgow firm failed for 2 millions. On 27th Oct. the L'pool Borough Bank suddenly and unexpectedly failed. On the 4th November bank rate raised to 9 per cent which up to that time had been quite unprecedented. This proved to be a complete and thorough crisis – tho' not so bad in England as in America. It is supposed that these crises generally occur at intervals of 20 years in America 1839–57–77 have been made crises in America. In America restoration was slow and 1858–9 were periods of great depression and some of the states wh. were intending to make railways all over entirely collapsed.[5] But in England the restoration was rather rapid. So by the year 1861 we were in great prosperity again, partly due perhaps to the price of cotton. Then intervened a new circumstance, viz., the alteration of the laws concerning partnership. Limited liability was quite a new thing then and the passing of the acts upon that subject[6] led to a very considerable bubble. One of the acts was passed in 1862. It opened limited liability to all sorts and kinds of companies. The number of companies created was most extraordinary. In the 4 years 1863–6, 876 new companies were brought out and the total authorised capital was 373 millions. This is only the companies made public. In 1864, 282 companies were started. In 1865, 287; in 1866, only 44 companies, showing the enormous fluctuation in enterprise. The *interest** of this fluctuation was very much diminished by the fact that the American war naturally interfered with things, and brought the cotton famine and destroyed the normal course of fluctuation. But in other branches there was this *definite*† bubble. It also took the form of railway construction again, the practice having grown up of railways being projected by contractors for their own advantage.

Then in 1866 a crisis came like that of 1847 in which several of these

---

† ?   (H. R.)

[5] The banking crisis of 1857, an important turning-point in international financial development, began with the sudden depreciation of railway securities in America and the consequent suspension during October of nearly all the banks along the eastern seaboard. A large proportion of the capital which backed the American railway boom was held by British investors and the full impact of the crisis hit Britain at a time when economic anxiety was already heightened by the aftermath of the Crimean War, the Indian Mutiny and a succession of poor harvests. The first major failures were Macdonald & Co., Glasgow muslin producers, and the Liverpool Borough Bank. Scottish and Irish banks were under particular pressure and the drain on gold from London reduced the reserves held by the Bank of England to under £1.5 million. The situation was saved only by the suspension of the 1844 Act. See Clapham, *Bank of England*, II, 222–38; A. Feavearyear, *The Pound Sterling*, second edition (Oxford, 1963) pp. 291–7.

[6] Cf. Vol. II, Letter 88, p. 232, n. 8.

* ?   (H. R.)

† district?   (H. R.)

contractors were broken altogether. In the beginning of 1866 interest rose
to 8 per cent. In February joint stock discount companies failed. Then
Sab^n‡ a railway contractor. In April Barnett Bank, L'pool, broke for 3¼
millions. Then these crises always came in the spring or autumn. They
never occurred in winter. This occurred in spring instead of autumn – the
great collapse being in May – the 10th of May being the date of the
failure of Overends for 10 millions. They had been the centre of the
money market for the disposal of short dated capital and their breaking
down shook the whole market. Peto and Betts failed next day for 4
millions.[7] This proved to be a pretty complete collapse, but for two or
three years there was a depressed state of trade. Nothing like that in
1840's for instance, but the same phenomena.

But then began a great demand for iron and metals. That produced a
great pull upon the coal people. The miners took advantage of it to
shorten their hours of labour and restricted the output, and so the price
was run up to two or three times its ordinary rate.[8] That alone could not
have lasted and must have brought on a collapse of enterprise. But it was
complicated by the complete breakdown in America, which, I believe,
was precipitated by simply the collapse of the American paper money.
That had produced a high range of prices and high land rents.* Now,
when the paper was restricted and lessened in quantity, prices fell, but
they would not fall slowly. A fall of prices occurs upon the breakdown,
and that came in 1872 – very prematurely – very severe in America and is
not over yet.[9] No crisis in England worth speaking of.

‡ ?   (H. R.)   [Thomas Savin]
[7] The fall of Overend, Gurney & Co. was followed by a severe run on all banks. Among those
which failed to survive were Messrs Peto & Betts of London, and Barned's Banking Co. Ltd of
Liverpool, which had been established in 1809 and was suspended on 19 April 1866. See *Bankers'
Magazine*, 26 (1866) 545–6, 640, 682–96.
[8] Jevons was probably referring to a strike in the South Wales pits from January to May 1875 over
a 10 per cent cut in wages, in which the miners were forced to concede a 12½ per cent reduction. Until
the mid 1870s, wages were not a crucial issue in the mines. They were regulated according to the
price of coal, which fetched a steady 5 shillings per ton from 1865 to 1870. From 1871 to 1873 there
was a substantial increase in both production and price, which reached a peak of 7/6d in 1873. The
price fell by 2 pence in 1874, matched by a 2 million ton fall in production. In 1875 the price fell
further to 7 shillings, but output rose by almost 7 million tons to over 133 million. See J. R. Raynes,
Coal and its Conflicts (1928) pp. 36–7, 52–3.
*   ?   (H. R.)
[9] The American crisis of 1873–5 began with the collapse of the boom in rail construction in the
autumn of 1873, although, as Jevons observed, a decline had already begun in 1872 with a fall in
prices. For a full account, see Irwin Unger, *The Greenback Era* . . . (Princeton, 1964) pp. 213–85. Cf.
also Vol. IV, Letters 377 and 386, pp. 43 and 56.

LECTURE XXII

BANK OF ENGLAND AND MONEY MARKET GENERALLY*[1]

In consequence of the crisis Peel separated the bank into "issue department" and "banking department".

Account March 5/62.

The government debt. – a fixed quantity, only alters when other banks cease issuing.

As the securities and govt. debt are fixt in amount the total varies according to the arithmetical increase or decrease of the gold coin and bullion.

Looking at line C in issue department.

E follows almost the same course. The reason is that it is fixed and is the amount of the govt. debt.

D varies more slightly. It shows the amount in millions of Bank of England notes which are outside the bank of England. Now the note issue is $29\frac{1}{2}$ millions and is equal to the amt. shown in E.

Take "notes" from "notes issued" you get 21,530,950 wh. must be the amt. in the hands of the public represented by the line D.

This reserve is the amount of notes created and is shown in line G.

H represents private deposits. Add public deposits and you get to line J which goes up and down four times every year, due to the payment of the dividends and the national debt. Above that, notes and private securities.

---

* (There seems to have been a table on the board – or a diagram wh. I do not appear to have copied.) (H. R.)

[1] The diagram which Rylett did not copy was in fact Jevons's *Diagram showing all the Weekly Accounts of the Bank of England since the passing of the Bank Act of 1844* (1862). The Weekly Account of the Bank of England for the week ending 5 March 1862 was included in the explanatory notes published along with the *Diagram*. The diagram and notes were reprinted in the first edition of *Investigations*, pp. VIII – XV.

On the diagram the figures for the Issue Department were plotted in the lower part, those for the Banking Department in the centre and those for country banks at the top. The lines connecting the observations were lettered as follows:

[A – Lower Base Line]
 B – Bank Minimum Rate of Discount
 C – Gold Coin and Bullion
 D – Amount of Notes in the hands of the Public
 E – Total Amount of Notes out of Issue Department
[F – Base Line for Banking Department figures]
 G – Reserve of Notes
 H – Private Deposits
 J – Total Private and Public Deposits
 K – Notes and Private Securities
 L – Total Assets and Liabilities
[M – Base Line for Country Bank Circulation]
 N – Total Amount of Notes issued by Private Banks
 O – Total Amount of Notes issued by Private and Joint Stock Banks

In line C you see marked the financial crisis. In first 4 years, active years without difficulty. Bullion as high as 16 millions. Result of so much bullion was that there was a pretty fair reserve of notes in the banking department.

Amt. of bullion in issue department.	15,000,000
,, of securities.	14,000,000
	29,000,000
Notes in hand of Public (assumed).	24,000,000
Then notes in bank dept. will be	5,000,000

Then suppose bullion to have risen to 20 millions and securities remain the same, i.e. 14 millions = 34 millions.

Subtract notes in public hands = 24 millions

Subtracting notes in banking department 10 millions.

The "other deposits" – an expression for all deposits of money not made by government departments – amt. to $13\frac{3}{4}$ millions, and the notes amount to not quite 9 millions – consequence is that the amount of notes is not adequate to pay the deposits if demanded.

Looking at G we observe that it is subject to very great variations. It is moderately high during 1844–5–6 but in the year 1847 it sinks down in the spring to 2,560,000 and then again in Autumn it sinks down to 1,180,000. Then this reserve of notes is totally inadequate to meet the liabilities of the bank. Looking a little above you observe a line of total deposits which amounted to something like 15 millions so that the bank had liabilities of at least 15 millions but only a reserve of one million and a little more.

Then during 1848 and 51 the reserve of notes was adequate – about 10 millions.

Then we come to that time when gold diggings had their effect and there is therefore a rise in gold coin and bullion. If you look at line C you see in 1851 it fell down something like 13 millions. Then it rapidly rose until in 1852 it was nearly 22 millions. I think that is about the highest amount it has ever been – when it amounted to 24 or 25 millions. The effect of this great accumulation of gold in 1852 was to occasion a rise in the reserve of notes, which rose on June 29th to a maximum of 14,240,000. This amount of gold existing in the country necessarily had the effect of increasing prices, and from what I showed you the other day there was a considerable rise in prices. And that rise in prices had the effect of increasing the amount of notes used by the public. As you see the amt. of notes in the hands of the public rose to 23 or 24 millions – the highest it has ever been. Then if you look below you see at bottom of all, B, a black line in interrupted straight portions that indicate the bank rate, and that shows the cost of borrowing money at short periods. Then you observe that when the amt. of the reserve is high this is low. In 1852 it fell as low as 2 per cent. In 1844–45 2½ p.c. Then from 1849 to the early part of 1853 there was a low rate of discount, and it is in these periods of low discount that trade takes its rise. Following that we see the brisk trade of 1853 produces a rise, and that thro' the action of the exchanges – wh. we find high prices – encouraged imports and discouraged exports. That is shown by the continuous decrease of the gold coin and bullion line wh. fell from 1853 to 1854. Then as gold went away the reserve of notes decreased correspondingly, and as the reserve of notes decreased they charged more for little loans.

Then the war in Russia checked trade and we see that shown in the rise of gold coin and bullion in the middle of the year 1853. But still as the war terminated pretty soon and business continued pretty active, and then we have a high rate of discount through 1856 and 57 when there was a great crisis in America. And looking at the reserve of notes, we find that in the autumn of 1856 it fell 2½ millions, and there was a rise of the rate of discount to seven per cent. But because there had been no panic in America there was none here. Then in the spring of 1857 there was a fall down to 3 millions again, and here you will observe these great falls in the reserve of notes almost always happening either in spring or autumn. In the autumn it fell to less than 1 million and there was a great crisis in the U. States. The consequence was there was a crisis in England. The rate rose to 10 per cent in a run of a week or two. A crisis occurred in Nov. 1857 and the government had to promise to support the bank in breaking the bank charter act. Now, the suspension of the bank charter act in England meant that they could issue notes irrespective of the amount of gold and on this occasion they did so, with no corresponding alteration in the gold coin and bullion (a little dip at the end of 1857 – that represents the amount of notes issued in defiance of the law.)* Then the effect of this freedom of issuing notes was to produce confidence in all the merchants and bankers that they could pay their debts if it came to the worst, i.e. the bank would lend them money to tide over difficulty.

Then, for several years, there was an abundance of money. The rate fell 3 p. ct. to 2½ p. ct. until in 1861 there was pressure and the rate rose to 8 per ct.

It is also worthy of notice that each of these crises has resulted in the decrease of private and joint stock notes. After 1847 and 57 there was a sudden decrease of them in lines O. N. together with a slight increase previously. But they are restricted to the amt. they may issue.

* ? (H. R.)

GENERAL CHARACTER OF A CREDIT CYCLE.

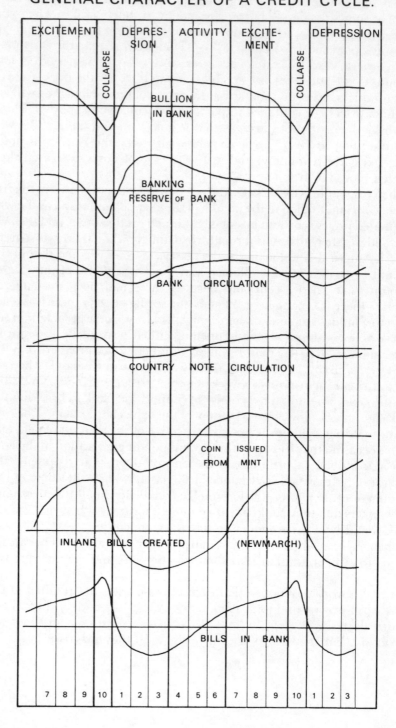

GENERAL CHARACTER OF A CREDIT CYCLE

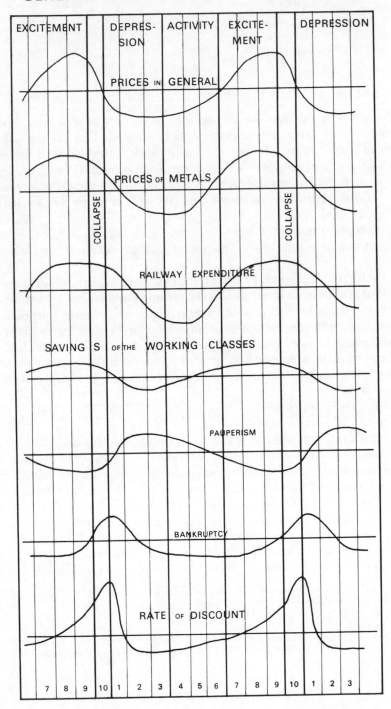

EXCITEMENT	DEPRES-SION	ACTIVITY	EXCITE-MENT	DEPRESSION

PRICES IN GENERAL

PRICES OF METALS

COLLAPSE

COLLAPSE

RAILWAY EXPENDITURE

SAVING S OF THE WORKING CLASSES

PAUPERISM

BANKRUPTCY

RATE OF DISCOUNT

7 8 9 10 1 2 3 4 5 6 7 8 9 10 1 2 3

See John Mill's [*sic*] paper in the M'Chester Statistical Society's proceedings for 1867.[2]

LECTURE XXIII

TAXATION

Taxation is altogether a different sort of subject in this sense – being altogether a matter of appointment to be judged of by the state in the form of a deliberate scheme; whereas in almost the whole of the other parts of political economy we are investigating natural growths. Trade etc. goes on best when left alone. Now taxation is necessary because no one would naturally tax themselves. At any rate the results wd. be naturally small if they did. But again it may be said that tho' taxation is arbitrary, results are not, but you cannot make them not feel the results and not in free industry as a consequence/*of that** taxation in a particular way.

I should have liked to ask what is the function of taxation, what are the limits of government interference. On the one hand we hold that absolute freedom of trade is desirable except so far as revenue purposes are concerned. But you cannot hold any doctrine of that sort with entire absoluteness i.e. you must always check the freedom of individuals by some state action adopted to prevent abuses – and the great question arises where exactly you must draw the line between good and evil results of freedom.

1st. Necessary functions:

2nd. Optional functions:

The necessary functions include all things absolutely necessary for the existence of the state. The most primitive of these is outward defence. It is often war with other states which binds people together in common action. 2nd repression of crime, wh. really is securing freedom of individuals. Kant laid down a kind of moral axiom that every one was so to act that other people were to be free to act in the same way;[1] but that almost [*is*] a self evident axiom – which must be true. But of course it is obvious that crimes cannot be included in that, because it would be self destructive. Closely connected with that comes courts of justice, and the

---

[2] This diagram was in fact taken by Jevons from the paper by John Mills – 'On Credit Cycles and the Origin of Commercial Panics', *Transactions of the Manchester Statistical Society for the Session 1867–68*, pp. 5–40. See Vol. III, Letter 273, n. 1, p. 140.

* -or "hold"   (H. R.)

[1] Immanuel Kant, *Fundamental Principles of the Metaphysic of Morals* (1785). See *Kant's Critique of Practical Reason and other Works on the Theory of Ethics*, translated by Thomas Kingsmill Abbott (1873; sixth edition 1909) p. 38.

maintenance of contracts: civil law, as compared with criminal law; but tho' the laws of England draw a very marked line between criminal and civil cases, they graduate very much into one another.

The optional functions include care of the highways. That in certain primitive or newly settled countries is almost requisite on the part of a country. The great highways in this country are not provided by the government. But in the colonies they are, and in many foreign states partly or wholly so. Provision of money, post office, defining weights and measures, surveying the country and so forth – all these may be called optional functions of government.

I must particularly point out that there is really no definite end to the functions of govt. and that the progress of legislation seems to lead to a great extension e.g. govt. provides libraries and museums, and undertakes to observe the weather and there is hardly any limit to the number of things which the govt. may usefully undertake to provide, when the public utility of these things is exceedingly obvious and when it is plain that they can be more cheaply and effectively done by a single agency.

The fact is the whole question turns upon this: whether a single monopoly in this case is best or whether the competition of individual firms is best. There are advantages about a monopoly, and disadvantages. In former years it was a great absurdity in London that many of the streets had a whole series of gas pipes all down them, and were being continually turned up and separately repaired, and then it was observed that one pipe would be better. That question is really being decided at the present time because many towns like Manchester are supplying their own gas.

The truth on this subject I should say is that there is no general principle, except that of adding up the comparative advantages in each particular case, i.e. you must make the best observation you can of the results of experiments one way or the other.

The Manchester Omnibus Company ought to be in the hands of the local government.

What I have stated is Mill's result.[2]

The inconvenience of govt. action is that it involves the raising of taxation in many cases. There are cases where industry undertaken by govt. pays itself. The Post Office returns considerable revenue to the govt., and yet does the work generally speaking cheaper than individuals could do it, but not always. But of course there are a great many other things that cannot be made to pay by those who derive the benefit. Indeed there are so many departments of govt. not self supporting that we require much taxation.

[2] Mill, *Principles*, book v, chapter xi, §§ 11 and 16, pp. 954–6, 970–1.

Now in the raising of taxation you cannot lay down any definite principle. The case is very much like what I have suggested as regards the function of govt., i.e. that there is no single principle of taxation, and cannot be: that throughout it is nothing but a balancing of particular advantages and disadvantages. And these advantages have to be calculated in the case of every individual tax. And then again there is another complication, that some taxes may form a complement to other taxes as it were, that even if a tax be undesirable in itself, it may be desirable for the purpose of equalising taxation or balancing some other tax. Thus, altogether anything like dogmatising in taxation is wrong.

It is by no means true that taxation is proposed for one purpose only.

1. The amount of revenue raised is the most obvious and important ground of taxation.

2. The moral effect of taxation in repressing consumption. Very little is said about that in the present day and it is supposed we have almost abandoned the idea of sumptuary taxes. In former times we imposed taxes upon silk dresses or long shoes. But the large part of our revenue is raised upon this principle: e.g. the taxation upon alcoholic liquors.[3] The enormous sum raised from this can only be justified upon moral grounds.

3. In former times in this country and in other countries at present there used to be a great tendency to look to the industrial effects of taxation, i.e. protection.

   The fallacies of protection seem to be dominant in many parts of the world. A pamphlet from Carey of America has been sent us.[4]

4. Slight incidental motives – that might be summed up as incidental.

One by no means unfortunate result of taxation is the statistics gained. We should know very little about trade if it were not for the custom houses. We should have to keep up the custom houses for statistics if for no other reason.

We will now look at four maxims of taxation which Adam Smith laid down as to the qualities proper in a tax. They have been repeated by every political economist, and may be considered classical. They are not at all exhaustive, but still nobody can deny the importance of them. They are the maxims of *Equality, Certainty, Convenience,* and *Economy.*[5]

---

[3] The annual yield of taxes on beer, wine and spirits increased from about £18 million in 1815 to over £30 million in 1881. See S. Dowell, *A History of Taxation and Taxes in England*, 4 vols (1884) II, 248, 396. Cf. also W. S. Jevons, 'On the Pressure of Taxation', *Principles of Economics* (1905) pp. 253–64.

[4] Henry Charles Carey, Philadelphia publisher and advocate of protection. Cf. Vol. III, Letter 311, n. 4, p. 201. Jevons was probably referring to Carey's pamphlet *Commerce, Christianity and Civilization versus British Free Trade. Letters in reply to the London Times* (Philadelphia, 1876).

[5] Smith, *Wealth of Nations*, book v, chapter II, part II; II, 310–12.

I.   Subjects of every state ought to support the government as nearly as possible to their respective abilities.

That is a statement which admits of much discussion. It lies at the basis of the subject of taxation and cannot be said to be at all settled. Here Smith says that everybody should pay in proportion to the revenue wh. they respectively enjoy under the protection of the state, i.e. everybody should pay a uniform share of their income. That is a doubtful proposition theoretically, and must be looked at from many sides. Would you say first of all whether you think it fair for everybody?

Now suppose taxation all round is 10 per cent.

£100 a year would be £10 for the government.

£1,000 a year would be £100 for the government.

£10,000 a year would be £1,000 for the government.

The result may be thus shown:

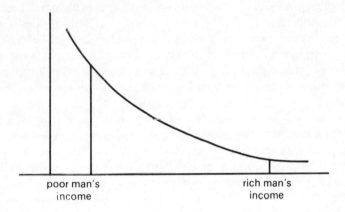

poor man's income   rich man's income

Thus the poorer man does suffer more than the richer, because the richer man's additional income represents the short line i.e. the taxation only bears a very small real proportion to his total income compared with the proportion which the poor man's taxation bears to his.

(The general idea gathered from the conversational illustration of the diagram was that £10 was of more importance to a man whose income was only £100 a year than £100 would be to a man whose income is £1,000; and of *vastly more* importance than £1,000 wd. be to a man whose income was £10,000 a year.)

I don't mean to say I should take that beyond theory. The practical side of the question may be very different from the theoretical side, and there arises this difficult question at once: if you depart from a pro-rata taxation what other rate are you to establish. There is no means of knowing any other: and that is one objection to abandoning perfect equality.

Another objection is this: that if you begin to exempt the poorer classes you exempt by far the most numerous part of the population, and those who have an immense predominance of voting power, so that it approximates to 99 out of the community taxing the 100th. Supposing that to go on there would arise a very serious objection, that large taxation upon the very wealthy wd. tend immensely to decrease the accumulation of capital in the country and in that way would affect the progress and prosperity of the whole; so that a very serious doubt arises whether on the whole progressive taxation in the proportion of income wd. not on the whole be much worse than the equality recommended by Smith. My impression is that upon the whole it is best to keep Adam Smith's equality of ratio.

But in our present system the question hardly arises because the poorer classes in England pay almost nothing at all except thro' customs duties e.g. on alcoholic liquors. But if a man is a teetotaler and does not smoke he pays hardly any taxation, provided indeed he does not keep a dog and doesn't write many letters. If he writes letters he pays a halfpenny on each. But it is very difficult to point out any taxes a working man pays. He may sometimes require a receipt stamp. Indirectly therefore they may pay taxes.

II. The second is the maxim of certainty. The tax which each individual is bound to pay ought to be certain and not arbitrary. Time of payment and manner of payment ought to be clearly stated. These are of great importance. Nothing paralyses industry so much as the feeling that property is at the mercy of the tax gatherer. Turkey is the best possible instance.

But this maxim applies to certain important cases of taxes which still remain. One important rule of finance in this Kingdom is that all duties should be levied according to bulk or weight, and not, as it is said *ad valorem*. An *ad valorem* tax means one that is proportionate to the value of the substance taxed. Silk varies in value. Tea varies in value from a few pence a pound to two shillings a pound wholesale, or more than that. But the tax levied by the custom house is uniform upon all – so much per pound. Now upon what ground can we justify that? As a rule the finer qualities of things are used by the richer classes and following the maximum of equality we ought to tax them at least according to price. Nevertheless Mr. Gladstone fixed that all taxes should be in proportion to bulk or weight simply on the ground of this maxim – that it is the only certain way of defining what is to be paid. [6] If you put the duty *ad valorem*,

[6] Peel's tariff revision of 1842, which abolished the *ad valorem* principle, had the effect of reducing the number of articles liable to duty from over twelve hundred to seven hundred and fifty. The Act of

the discretion of the tax gatherer comes in as to what the value is, and great chances of fraud are opened up.

New South Wales a few years ago established high *ad valorem* duties. After a few years it worked so badly that they have given it up. Is this fair? The answer is that nobody uses nothing but silk and wine, that everybody pays on the number of things and therefore it does not follow that a rich man's taxation on the whole is unfair, for the aggregate burdens a man, and not individual items.

III.   Thirdly the maxim of convenience. Every tax ought to be levied in the time and amount in which it is most likely to be convenient to the contributor to pay it. Everybody agrees to this at first sight, and it is so far true in that a government generally is much more able to wait for their money or to modify the mode of receipt than the individual. Most people think, and probably justly, that Mr. Lowe committed an offence against this maxim when he insisted that everybody should pay income tax immediately after Xmas.[7] He did it upon the ground that it was convenient to get all the income tax in that quarter, so that the total revenue might be made up before the 1st of April, and then the Budget could be brought forth and all the facts brought forward at the proper time. It would be most convenient to the Chancellor of the Exchequer. Then, ought it, or ought it not to be done?

After all, however, it is a matter of small importance for the government to get money, and so to put any chance of pressure upon the money market merely for the convenience of the Budget seems to me unnecessary.

One of the best taxes in this point of view is the penny stamp for receipts. I don't hear anybody object to that tax except myself.

IV.   The fourth maxim is that every tax ought to be so contrived as both to take out and keep out of the pockets of the people as little as possible over and above what it brings into the public treasury.

The actual cost of collecting taxes varies immensely from almost nothing up to several times the amount of the tax. The most costless of all

---

the Tariff, 1842 (5 & 6 Vict. c. 47) reduced duties on manufactured and partially manufactured goods, at a cost of £1.2 million to the Exchequer. The laborious task of carrying out the reform fell on Gladstone, then a junior minister. He later published a pamphlet on his experiences, *Remarks upon Recent Commercial Legislation* (1845). See John Morley, *The Life of William Ewart Gladstone*, 3 vols (1903) I, 251–9; Dowell, *History of Taxation*, II, 306.

   [7]   Robert Lowe, while Chancellor of the Exchequer in the Gladstone Administration of 1868–74, introduced an important tax reform in his first budget of 1869, when he abolished half-yearly collection in July and January, in favour of an annual collection on 1 January. The principle of raising revenue for the year within the year was therefore established and maintained, despite strong opposition, in the 1871 budget, when Lowe was forced to drop the proposed Match Tax, which Jevons supported: cf. below, p. 138. See Dowell, *History of Taxation*, II, 354–6, 363–7; also Vol. III, Letter 328, n. 1, p. 231.

taxes are those which are simply levied by accounts, as for instance the former duty upon railway travelling – because these are simply taxes paid for by public companies upon the results of their year's account. The income tax is a very fair instance of a costly tax.

The taxes to wh. objection may fairly be made on this ground are the customs duties. Not only do they require a very costly system of custom house supervision and large staff of excise officers and altogether a very expensive government department but beyond that they produce a great deal of burden upon the public in the shape of interest upon money which is for the time being invested in taxes. Then they occasion a great deal of trouble to the dealers in these articles, and all this put together makes a burden upon the public a very considerable consideration. The mere increase of interest upon the tax amounts from ten to twenty per cent. But then a great many points have to be remembered in considering this.

The income tax for instance applies only to a small class, and if it were got from workmen it might be far more expensive even than the customs department. The consequence is that according to the English system at present the rich are taxed by the income tax and certain others. The poor are taxed by the custom houses or by the excise officers.

These maxims hardly cover the whole question and upon pages six and seven of the pamphlet (on Taxation) I have suggested as many as ten heads. [8]

1. Fraudulent evasion.
2. Non fraudulent evasion.
3. Costliness of collection as regards government.
4. [Costliness to the public in money.]
5. Loss of time and trouble on the part of the public.
6. Interference with home trade.
7. Interference with foreign trade.
8. Unpopularity.
9. Incidental objections.
10. Inadequacy of returns.

If you take any particular tax the question must be resolved by considering each of these. What would you say as to such an inconsiderable tax as the dog tax as regards fraudulent evasion?

Taxation generally is an immensely wide subject and it wd. be impossible to give more than a very few ideas about it, and in England to a great extent the questions of taxation have been replaced and done away with by the great reforms effected by Peel and Gladstone. In old books upon Political Economy you come upon questions of sliding scales etc., the very meaning of which is forgotten by the present generation. In

[8] W. S. Jevons, *The Match Tax: A Problem in Finance. Principles of Economics*, pp. 209–50. The pamphlet was first published in 1871.

the beginning of the century, being impressed with the necessity of fighting France and some other countries of Europe duties were imposed upon almost everything. At one time there would be thousands of articles in the tariff. Then the gradual progress of reform was directed by certain definite principles, one of which was to reduce the number of articles taxed at different times in England.

1660 there were 1630 articles taxed.

1787   ,,   ,,   1425   ,,   ,,
1826   ,,   ,,   1280   ,,   ,,
1841   ,,   ,,   1052   ,,   ,,

Then came the great reform of Peel, and I must say that the fact is that Gladstone, all the time throughout the measures of Mr. Peel, was engaged with him as under secretary, and it is difficult to say how far the reforms of Peel may have been made in conjunction with Gladstone.

In 1849 there were 515 articles taxed. Then Gladstone established the following principles:

1st. that unproductive duties should be done away with altogether. i.e. if some very little article scarcely used brings in no amount of any consequence then it is much simpler to do away with it altogether.

2nd. That there should be no duties upon raw materials. The tax should be upon the finished article or articles for immediate consumption as far as possible, because if you tax raw material – say you tax timber, e.g. timber used in making a piano – that timber has to be kept several years before it can be used. Then the owner is paying interest or has sunk his capital in this stock in trade and therefore the ultimate price of the piano must be raised. Accordingly all the duties upon raw materials were done away with as quietly as possible and those which now remain are not upon raw materials.

3.   They were to be not *ad valorem*. The result of carrying out these reforms was that only 19 or 20 articles were retained. In 1829 it was discovered that of 25 millions of customs duties 20 millions were returned by 20 articles and the remaining few millions by 400 articles. Then Gladstone made the important step of doing away with the 400 and thus freeing trade. Several of the remainder have since been removed – corn, timber, sugar, silk, so that now we simply have perhaps not more than six articles taxed, i.e. spirits, wine, tea, coffee, tobacco, dried fruits, gold and silver plate.

Of course the extent of taxation with regard to other countries is very different from this in England. That in America is governed by difft. principles.

Indirect and *Direct*.

Direct means paid by the person upon whom the incidence of the tax falls.

Indirect taxes are those paid by one person and transferred to the shoulders of another person in the manner of customs duties, but the fact is that to draw a very accurate line is difficult to do.

The whole subject is one of rough approximation and depends upon the theory of probabilities.

One idea is, don't reduce them too much in number.